BRAHMINISM

BRAHMINISM

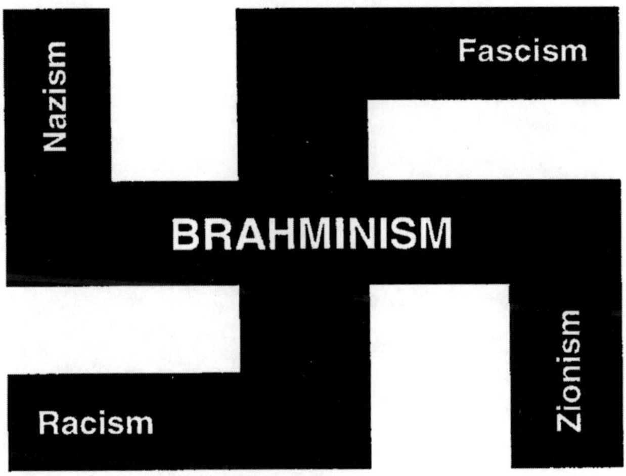

V.T. Rajshekar

DALIT SAHITYA AKADEMY
109/7th Cross, Palace Lower Orchards,
Bangalore - 560 003 India

First Edition : 1981

Second Edition : 1994

Third Revised & Enlarged Edition : 2002

Price: Rs. 50 in India

US $ 5 (Outside India)

Front cover picture: Courtesy *Deccan Herald*

Printed at:
St. Paul Publications
8th Mile, Tumkur Road
Nagasandra P.O.
Bangalore - 560 073

The book is
dedicated to our
darling baby
TASHI
who is fast
shaping herself
to step into
our shoes
and getting
intellectually
equipped to combat
the virus of
Brahminism
crippling India

CONTENTS

PREFACE TO THE THIRD EDITION

Ever heard of lambs loving the wolf? Anywhere in the world?

Seven Wonders of the World are all well known. But none has added another to this stand-still list though the Eighth Wonder of the World has been existing in India since centuries without being noticed by ordinary eyes. That is the greatness of the Eighth Wonder.

What is this Eighth Wonder that exists only in India? What is the greatness of this wolf being loved by its innocent victims?

The book deals with this mysterious creature that goes unnoticed. Such is the greatness of this elusive animal.

That wolf is Brahminism — loved, adored, worshipped and even carried on the head by all the victims of its hate philosophy and crimes.

To our knowledge this is perhaps the only book in English to come out in the past 20 years or so on this subject. This is because the wolf is fully disguised and puts on a show of caring and sharing. If lambs outside India are victims of violence here they are victims of non-violence. God's name on the tongue but dagger under the armpit.

There used to be lots of writings on this subject and lots of discussions during pre-independence days and for sometime even after that. Eminent Brahmins themselves used to be harsh on Brahminism. But as days passed Brahminism gradually dried up the country's intellectual oasis. Today, India is a vast intellectual desert. Poverty of thinking is so much that every "eminent" writer keeps off this forbidden subject for his survival.

Brahminism is an unique social institution in the world because by nature it stunts the growth of people, encouraging utter intellectual poverty and also dishonesty. No section of the population is spared from this pestilence. Brahmins themselves have been victims of Brahminism. But the wonder is they don't want to know that.

India's literate population itself is too small. It has almost stopped growing. The English-knowing elite (cream) is not even 2% of its 1,000 million population. This minuscule minority of 2%, comprising mostly the wolves themselves, wants to pose and pass off as the greatest lovers of the lambs. The leadership outside this charmed circle of wolves is corrupted and co-opted, living on the mercies of the wolves. Quite some lambs have even developed tendencies of the wolf.

Hence the subject of Brahminism has become a prohibited area for this mercenary class of lambs. The subject is never discussed in public. Not even in academic circles. Those who dare rake up the subject are mercilessly dealt with. That is why everybody plays safe for fear of being ostracized.

The urbanised, educated elites continue to be the most ignorant lot living in their own fool's paradise. India's intellectual desert is fast expanding.

Brahminism may be the ruling class philosophy, yielding high profits to its practitioners, but over 85% of the country's population — victims of this philosophy — will never, ever accept it. If the rulers try to impose it on the unwilling lambs not only the process (called *hinduisation*) will be too painful but there is every chance of this multi-national country breaking up. The Gujarat genocide of Muslims in the year 2002 has proved how painful is this *hinduisation* process.

However unpopular and unpleasant the subject of Brahminism may be, if a writer wants to be guided by his conscience and wants to establish his intellectual honesty, he or she has to tackle it - and pay the price for speaking out the Truth. We are fulfilling exactly that responsibility.

And in doing so we are proud that we are following the footsteps of India's greatest revolutionaries like Budha, Guru

Nanak, Basaveshwara, Mahatma Phule, Sri Narayana Guru, Periyar E.V. Ramaswamy, Dr. Ram Manohar Lohia and more than anybody else Dr. Babasaheb B.R. Ambedkar who spent his whole life fighting the wolves and rescuing the innocent lambs.

We are fully aware of the "controversy" this book will generate. Over-fed wolves feeding on innocent lambs will not tolerate any threat to its uninterrupted free meal. Particularly when Brahminism for the first time in history has started jumping on the world stage following the Sept.11, 2001 "terrorist" attack on USA, manipulating world opinion and joining the "Triangle of Tyrants".

When the country's ruling class itself is subjected to surgery will it tolerate the pain? But the surgeon can't be blamed for the disease that necessitated the surgery.

We have no ill-will against any individual member of the Brahminical Social Order. The surgery is intended to dissect the system, rescue the lambs — as well as the wolf. The book deals with this hitherto unknown Eighth Wonder of the World.

Bangalore
June 1, 2002

V.T. Rajshekar

PREFACE TO THE SECOND EDITION

Almost the entire thinking sections of India and abroad are now realising that India is still poor and ridiculed in the world outside because of Brahminism. To this day nobody has come out with a scholarly argument to elaborate this point.

No amount of economic development of India can change its position. Its proverbial poverty is not because of economic reasons but social, cultural factors having its roots in Brahminism. Many marxist scholars are also falling in line with this thinking.

Brahminism, which is the scientific name for Hinduism, is not a religion like Christianity, Islam or Budhism. It is an ideology. Those who subscribe to this ideology may be born Brahmins or even non-Brahmins like Kshatriyas, Vaishyas and some top landed *shudra* castes. In fact, some non-Brahmin castes are better practitioners of Brahminism than the Brahmins who are its prime promoters. Even some Untouchables and Tribals are getting brahminised. The cancer is spreading. But whether they be Brahmins or non-Brahmins, nobody has gained by holding on this anti-human ideology except that it helps the strong to exploit the weak.

Brahmins themselves at their many conferences and newspaper articles have been complaining of poverty and neglect. That means even after holding on to this ideology for thousands of years and selling it to everybody else, its very manufacturers have made no profit. What an accursed product.

Brahmins, who consider themselves superior to all others in India, have not been benefited by their own ideology. Women, including the Brahmin women, have been the worst victims of this ideology. Hence not only in the interest of India but even in the interest of Brahmins, its chief promoters, this ideology has to be destroyed. Such a task is not possible through election-oriented parliamentary or presidential system of government.

The war against Brahminism has to be fought outside the legislature. Because it cannot be abolished through legislation. The war against Brahminism must first begin in our minds, then in homes and then spill over to the streets and then sweep the country. Better to restrict our efforts to each "nation" within India instead of considering India as one nation. A cultural revolution to uproot Brahminism is the need of the hour.

The success of this book proves that a large section in India is coming to accept our viewpoint.

The war against Brahminism must get priority over all other issues. Without destroying the principal Enemy, we can't think of combating lesser evils.

We call upon those who are convinced of the urgent need to destroy Brahminism to save India not to stop at that but go forward and act. Ideas must lead to action. We are here to support you.

Bangalore (India)
Sept. 15, 1984.

V.T. Rajshekar

PREFACE TO FIRST EDITION

This monograph comes at a "critical" time in the history of India. In fact, no year goes without our leaders describing it as critical. That means as years pass, the country is sliding from one crisis to bigger crisis — social and economic. Not that we lack expertise. The country's "intellectuals" and "experts" are fully aware of the gravity of the situation. It is these "intellectuals" and "experts" who express "worry" about India's dash towards decay. And yet why no one wants to diagnose the disease and cure it? This is what is worrying us and the world outside. Our "intellectuals" and "experts" know what the disease is and still they do not want to cure it. Is there any greater treachery than this? Can we find a set of intellectuals and experts more dishonest than this?

The monograph is intended to expose the heartlessness of this tiny coterie — about 10% of our population — that controls the country. There is no malice, no ill-will or hatred against anybody. We love India and want India to have a revolution. Therefore, as a writer it is our duty to point out the hurdles in the way of that revolution. For this we have to speak out the truth. And what is the truth? The truth is that Brahminism is the bane of India. If India has to live, Brahminism has to die. And this world's most dangerous philosophy is practised not merely by Brahmins but also by a large number of non-Brahmins as well.

This is the truth and if truth hurts, we cannot help it. We are sure our sincere efforts at establishing truth will be appreciated by all those who love India.

Owing to overwhelming demands we developed our speech at the inauguration of the "Anti-Brahmin Domination Conference" conducted by the Dravida Kazhagam at Coimbatore in November 1980. The DK headed by K. Veeramani gave us the privilege of inaugurating two such mammoth conferences, the first one at Tirunelveli. That such conferences have had its desired effect can be made out from the front-page report published by all the South Indian editions of the country's biggest English chain, the *Indian Express* (Dec.31, 1980). K. Sriram, its reporter, referred to the "first signs of organised Brahmin power on Dec. 21, 1980 when thousands marched in procession from Mambalam (where the community reigns strong) to the Raj Bhavan in Madras. Later the reporter rightly gave the credit for provoking the Brahmin anger to K. Veeramani and the "denigration campaign" by the DK.

Clash of ideas is a must if the society has to become mobile. The Hindu society is a stagnant, stinking pool of water because there has been no discussion. That at least a section of the Brahmins in Tamil Nadu is forced to take to the streets proves that the efforts of the DK at churning the stagnant pool has succeeded. The monograph is intended to step up this churning process.

We are grateful to the *Indian Express* for not only pleading the Brahmin cause but also publishing (Jan.14, 1981) an article by a Brahmin, R. Sampath, who told the Brahmins:

> Why there should be a raging Brahmin phobia... The Brahmin, who was once expected not to think of his next meal, became greedy and a pest... falling from the heights of selflessness to the abysmal depths of self-aggrandizement, they naturally became alienated from other communities... The Brahmins turned their back on the code that governed the true Brahmin and started exploiting the ignorant and the gullible people".

We are thankful to R. Sampath for speaking out the truth.

This, incidentally, is the first publication of the Dalit Sahitya Akademy established with Dr. Mulk Raj Anand as the chief patron early in 1981.

Bangalore (India)

17-2-1981. **V.T. Rajshekar**

I - Is Social Justice Possible Without Destroying Brahminism?

Comrade Veeramani, General Secretary of the Dravida Kazhagam, Madras, and friends,

This is the second conference (1980) of its kind that you have called upon me to inaugurate. It looks as if Periyar E.V. Ramaswamy's followers in Tamil Nadu have fallen in love with me. I am getting a lot of invitations from your state. Tamil Nadu is the most virile state in the whole country. Dravidians were once the rulers of this land. Tamil was then the language of the whole sub-continent. Your Tirunelveli conference was a massive one. I was very much impressed by the organisational capacity and the discipline of the Dravida Kazhagam (DK). Hundreds of women formed the vanguard of the procession at Tirunelveli. The presence of women in such large numbers is of great historic significance. Every temple and Brahmin locality at Tirunelveli was guarded by the police.

I witnessed similar scenes at Coimbatore also as I walked in the procession. To that extent, Brahmins had got frightened. I read in the paper that several Brahmin organisations had demanded that this Coimbatore conference and procession be banned by the government. How silly. Why should anything be banned? Everybody must have equal opportunity to express his views. It is for the people to judge who is right and who is wrong. Only cowards are afraid of opposition.

The presence of women in such large numbers in the procession denouncing (Hindu) god, religion and the havoc caused by Brahminism was a fantastic sight. Mao had said women should form the vanguard of any revolutionary movement and then only it will succeed. If in India every movement is failing, it is because women are not taking a prominent part in such revolutionary causes. Men have suppressed them. Because religion told them so. The DK has to be congratulated for inspiring the women to lead the procession.

Tamil Nadu has been traditionally the leader of social revolution in India. Periyar E.V. Ramaswamy was the father of this movement. We, from Karnataka and those in the rest of India, have to learn a lot from you Tamilians. We look upon you for leadership. (*cheers*).

Why attack only Brahmins?

This question is now and then raised before us and you too will face similar queries. We want to make it clear that we have nothing against individual Brahmins. We also want to make it equally clear that ours is not a crusade against a single community — our war is against Brahminism which is more dangerous than the Brahmins. As the authors and custodians of "Sacred Scriptures", the Brahmins were the founders of Brahminism. So, individual Brahmins are not our enemies. If any individual Brahmin thinks that he is "hurt" by our criticism, we can only pity his ignorance.

Brahminism has not helped at least a sizeable section of Brahmins themselves. Some vocal Brahmins are fond of saying that a large number of Brahmins are poor. And many Brahmins are slogging as cooks, *archakas* (priests), clerks, teachers etc. The *Vedas, Upanishads*, the *Gita* and the elaborate rituals which the Brahmins prescribe to others to get-rich-quick has not helped even them — their very creators. We pity these ignorant Brahmins who themselves are the victims of Brahminism. Let the Brahmins save themselves first before they trap others. We admit that Brahmins are as much part of India as others. Therefore, we who fight Brahminism are equally interested in saving the "poor" Brahmins from the clutches of Brahminism. If they are wise, let them heed our warning. If not, they will have to face the fury of the masses.

We are often questioned as to why we attack only Brahmins and why not exploiters in every other caste and community? Why they alone are hated? Why only Brahmins are singled out for attack from Kashmir to Kanyakumari? Why more and more films, novels, poems, books and articles are coming portraying Brahmins alone as the blood-suckers and the greatest villains? Why the whole country is unanimous on this one subject? Why? Are they all mad to attack only Brahmins? What has gone wrong with them? Why is there such a chorus against Brahminism? The answer is simple: Brahminism is the other word for exploitation.

We will oppose exploitation by anybody, in any form. When we attack Brahminism, we are actually fighting against exploitation. Not Brahmins alone. This has to be clearly understood. That is why every movement for social justice in India since the days of Jainism and Budhism to the present-day took the form of anti-Brahminism. It is not Periyar and we alone who are running a crusade against Brahmins and Brahminism. As Jagjivan Ram said:

> "Any movement for social equality must be anti-Brahmin in character".

Vivekananda on Brahmins

Budha's was the first, the greatest and the most famous anti-Brahmin movement that practically wiped out Brahmins from this land. Similarly, every other social, cultural and religious movement in India was also anti-Brahmin in nature and content. Let the Brahmins who criticise us for singling out Brahmins for attack show us one single movement in India which was not anti-Brahmin in nature and content. Basaveshwara (Veerashaiva movement), Guru Nanak, Mahatma Phule, Sri Narayana Guru, Dr. Ambedkar, Periyar E.V. Ramaswamy, Lohia, Dalit Panthers or anybody else for that matter were all essentially anti-Brahmin.

Even Vivekananda and M.K. Gandhi, who cannot be accused of leading an anti-Brahmin crusade, did not have any good word for Brahmins. **Vivekananda** says:

> "They (Brahmins) began to arrogate powers and privileges to themselves. If a Brahmana killed a man, he would not be punished. The Brahmana, by his very birth, is the Lord of the Universe. Even the most wicked Brahmana must be worshipped."
>
> "Priestcraft is bane of the India" he says and asks people to "kick out the priests who are always against progress, because they would never mend". "A hundred million or so Brahmanas suck the blood of these poor people, without even the least effort for their amelioration — is that a country or a hell? Is that a religion or the devil's dance?" (*Caste, Culture and Socialism*, Swami Vivekananda, Advaita Ashrama, No.5 - Dehi Entally Road, Calcutta - 14, pp. 40 - 41).

Can we find a more devastating attack on Brahmins by the very high priest of the RSS, the country's most important Brahmin organisation?

Subramania Bharati, the most famous modern Tamil poet and himself a Smartha Brahmin, writes:

> It would pain me and, of course, it would pain others. If I should treat fully of all the makeshifts and devices whereby the Brahmanas of today attempt to preserve their totally undeserved claim for spiritual superiority. Now that India is awakening to a new Age, it will be well for my Brahmana countrymen if they voluntarily relinquish all their old pretensions together with the silly and anti-national customs based on such pretensions, and lead the way for the establishment of liberty, equality and fraternity among the Indians. (*New India*, May 11, 1915).
>
> The Brahmins are the sacerdotal caste of India. They are at the same time the proudest and the closest aristocracy that the world has ever seen, for they form not merely an aristocracy of birth in the strictest sense of the term, but are of divine origin. (*Indian Unrest*, **Valentine Chirol**, Macmilan & Co., London, 1910 p.32).
>
> **K. Srinivasa Rau** (himself a Desastha Brahman, a Marathi

speaker from Tanjore district) had for many years contended that India could not hope to develop politically until it closed the all too evident divisions in its society. In a book titled *The Present Political Unrest in India* (1908) he wrote: Unless the ground is cleared, the rocks and stones removed, the basis of National life broadened and deepened, and the centre of life and interests changed from persons to principles, and divergent sects, classes and creeds to the country at large, and unless our political sympathies go forth, from the pale of Iyers, Iyengars and Raus, to wider circles of men... transcending Brahman and non-Brahman... democracy on any large scale will be a danger, delusion and sham. (Eugene F. Irshick, *Politics and Social Conflicts in South India*, University of California Press, Berkeley and Los Angeles, 1969, pp.40-41).

M.K. Gandhi, who did everything to serve the Brahmins life-long and got the title of the Mahatma, also did not spare the Brahmins:

> "... Brahmins themselves have taught us to believe that they are the true custodians of the divine wisdom and that, where there is divine wisdom, there is no fear, there is no grinding pauperism, there is no high and low state, there is no greed, jealousy, war, plunder and the like. Because Brahminism went down, it drew down with it all the other classes of Hindus..." Elsewhere he says: "It is a pity that modern Brahmins not only pay no attention to the duties which have been laid down upon them and do not serve religion, but follow all manner of professions to enrich themselves". (*My Varnashrama Dharma*, Bharatiya Vidya Bhavan, Bombay-7, 1965 pp. 89 and 100).

Gandhi was right. According to the *Varnashrama Dharma*, the Brahmins had "reservations" only in learned professions. But today they are encroaching upon all those professions reserved by they themselves to the *shudras* and *ati-shudras*.

Despite such sincere, life-long service to Brahmins, Gandhi was finally shot down by a Brahmin himself. (V.T. Rajshekar: *Why Godse Killed Gandhi?*, DSA-1997).

Caste system destroyed India

Brahminism, which is the appropriate name for Hinduism, is nothing but the caste system. Minus caste, Hinduism is dead.

"If and when caste disappears from India, Hinduism will also disappear".

(M.N. Srinivas, *A Note on Sanskritisation and Westernisation — Far Eastern Quarterly,*. 1956 Vol.15 p.495).

This is the opinion of one who is considered India's top-most social scientist and himself a Brahmin. Caste system (*Varnasharama Dharma*) is the other name for Brahminism and this was denounced by many thinkers and reformers. As we have no time to give the opinion of non-Brahmins, we will confine only to those given by famous Brahmins.

Rabindranath Tagore:

The thing we in India have got to think of is this... to remove those social customs and ideals which have generated a want of self-respect and a complete dependence on those above us... a state of affairs which has been brought about entirely by the domination in India of the caste system, and the blind and lazy habit of relying upon the authority of traditions that are incongruous, anachronism in the present age.

Jawaharlal Nehru:

In the context of the society today, the caste system and much that goes with it are wholly incompatible, reactionary, restrictive and barriers to progress. There can be no equality in status and opportunity within its frame-work, nor can there be political democracy and much less economic democracy. Between these two conceptions conflict is inherent and only one of them can survive.

(*Discovery of India*, Chapter -VI, p. 234).

G.K. Gokhale:

The *Varnadharma* expressed a pyramidical society with each layer fixed and immovable thus making social revolution impossible.

(*Indian Thought Through the Ages*, 1961 p.36).

P.B. Gajendragadkar:

Social inequality and caste loyalty are totally inconsistent with secularism.

Brahmin & private property

Therefore, it's no wonder that all over India there has been a consistent crusade against Brahminism. And there is no movement in India, whether social, cultural or even religious, which was not basically anti-Brahmin in content. This point was underlined by N. Ram, no less a person than the editor of the *Hindu*, Madras, the most famous Brahmin English daily of India.

> In the modern colonial society, it was no surprise at all that any movement for social equality and against caste domination had to have an anti-Brahmin orientation....
>
> (*Economic & Political Weekly* Annual Number 1979, p. 379).

Those who fight for equality, social justice, destruction of private property, liberation of Dalits, emancipation of women etc. have to be essentially anti-Brahmin. One cannot be a supporter of Brahmins and also work for destruction of private property and socialism. If ever anybody practises such a deception in India (like our marxists) it can be considered as the biggest contradiction in Hindu India. Socialism will not come to India without destroying Brahminism. For further details please read the Bible of the RSS, *Bunch of Thoughts*, by Guru Golwalkar (Jagarana Prakashana, Kempegowda Nagar, Bangalore - 560 019, 1980, p.53).

No Brahmin can be revolutionary

Brahmins are opposed to any movement to abolish private property.

> Property is the severest limitation upon the mental and moral independence of man both in respect of thought and action. It produces a conflict for the two. That is why the Brahmin is always opposed to change. For, to him change means loss of power and loss of pelf.
>
> (Dr. Ambedkar, *The Buddha & His Dhamma*, Siddharth Publication, 1974, p. 317).

Therefore, no Brahmin can be a true and genuine revolutionary because even if he is a scientist, he can rarely get out of his caste cage, wedded as he is to status quo. There may be hundreds of Western-trained scientists. As Dr. Ambedkar said there may be any number of learned people among Brahmins but they have hardly produced any honest intellectual. Is it not a shame upon the community?

> The Brahmins form the vanguard of the movement for political reform and in some cases also of economic reform. But they are not to be found even as camp followers in the army raised to break-down the barricades of caste. Is there any hope of the Brahmins ever taking up a lead in the future in this matter? I say no. You may ask why? You may argue that there is no reason why Brahmins should continue to shun social reform. You may argue that the Brahmins know that the bane of the Hindu society is caste and as an enlightened class could not be expected to be indifferent to its consequences. You may argue that there are secular Brahmins and priestly Brahmins and if the latter do not take up the cudgels on behalf of those who want to break caste, the former will. All this of course sounds very plausible. But in all this, it is forgotten that the break of the caste system is bound to affect adversely the Brahmin caste. Having regard to this, is it reasonable to expect that the Brahmins will ever consent to lead a movement the ultimate result of which is to destroy the power and prestige of the Brahmin caste? Is it reasonable to expect the secular Brahmins to take part in a movement, directed against the priestly Brahmin? In my judgement, it is useless to make a distinction between the secular Brahmins and priestly Brahmins. Both are kith and kin. They are two arms of the same body and one is bound to fight for the existence of the other.
>
> (Dr. Ambedkar: *Annihilation of Caste*, Bheem Patrika Publications, April 1975, p. 87-88).

We need not read their Sacred Scriptures or consult experts to verify the truth of this statement that Brahmins are essentially status quoists.

The Rashtriya Swayamsevak Sangh (RSS) and its political party Jan Sangh, the biggest, the richest and the most famous organisation of Brahmins, was the first to oppose nationalisation of banks and any socialist measures in India. No

Shankaracharya has ever supported land reforms or nationalisation of urban property. On the other hand, the Satya Sai Baba, the most famous bum-licker of Brahmins, and every other godman like Chinmayananda, Rajneesh, etc. is firmly wedded to private property. To this day, we could hardly find a Brahmin of the stature of Dr. Ambedkar or Periyar who led a movement against private property.

That is why all Brahmins are so particular about private property. Says Saraswathi Menon in the *EPW*'s 1979 Annual No.:

> Throughout India, land ownership has usually been restricted to a few upper castes — in Thanjavur the *mirasi* system was linked to the sway of Brahmin landlordism... Brahmins, who formed little over six per cent of the district total population, held over 25 per cent of the ryot *pattas.* (p. 403).

On the other hand, those who opposed Brahmins like Periyar, Babasaheb Ambedkar, Lohia, Phule, Narayana Guru devoted their entire lifetime to destroy private property. It is they who were the real and genuine marxists and not the Danges, Namboodripads or P. Ramamurthys.

Not only that. The Brahmins were also opposed to equal rights to women. Even Jawaharlal Nehru, a "Socialist Brahmin", opposed Dr. Ambedkar's Hindu Code Bill conferring equal rights to women and that was the reason for the resignation of Dr. Ambedkar as the first Law Minister of India.

Nehru's bogus socialism

Nehru, who described himself as a socialist, could not get out of his Brahminism.

> Not many weeks after the Chinese launched their aggression, Nehru was in a mood to listen to the astrologer. But the Pandit's words were hardly comforting. Nehru's life span was over, they pronounced. Only *puja* (ritual worship) would prolong it. What followed was shrouded in utmost secrecy. Fifty learned priests were engaged by his admirers to perform the prescribed rites at a temple in Kalkaji, a suburb of Delhi. At the end of the daily ceremonies, the Brahmin Pandits repaired to place an

auspicious tilak mark on his forehead. Durga Das also narrates how a high official close to Nehru had revealed him something that lent weight to Sinha's.(Satya Narayan Sinha for several years Minister for Parliamentary Affairs) story of Nehru's gradual drift to queer beliefs. It is a peculiar oriental trait, this faith in soothsayers. Nehru, the iconoclast, fell prey to it in his last years.

(Durga Das: *India from Curzon to Nehru and After*).

So, those who oppose Brahminism are more sincere, dedicated in their words and deeds. On the other hand, the Brahmins and their institutions have been the greatest upholders of private property and inequality between man and man. Vedanta is the philosophy of the exploiting classes and we can verify this by looking at those attending Chinmayananda's discourses.

So, it can be scientifically proved that without destroying Brahminism, we cannot destroy private property. Brahminism and private property are the two sides of the same coin.

Marxist mischief

Look at all the property-holders in India — what we describe as the Big Business — Tatas, Birlas, Mafatlals, Sahu Jains, Bangurs, Kirloskars, Goenkas, Singhanias, etc. — all of them are the biggest supporters of Brahmins. They are the pillars of Brahminism. It is they who build new and newer temples (e.g. Birla Temple of Delhi) renovate the old and spend lavishly on all rituals. It is they who own the media and employ Brahmins or other upper caste journalists to run it. One is complimentary to the other. Banias (propertied class) want Brahmins and Brahmins want Banias. One cannot live without the other. It is this dangerous combination of "class" and "caste" that has made our problem doubly difficult. We have discussed it in our monograph, *How Marx Failed in Hindu India* (Dalit Sahitya Akademy - 1988) and also in *The Dilemma of the Class & Caste in India* (DSA -1984). Our marxists are thoroughly mistaken if they think they can destroy the propertied class without simultaneously destroying Brahminism. Brahminism is more dangerous than the private property. This is India's marxist mischief. They want to abolish private property without destroying Brahminism. Is this possible?

Enemy No.1 of Untouchables

Some Untouchables tell us that more than the Brahmins, it is the landed *shudras* who are the main perpetrators of violence on Untouchables. All over India, it is these *shudra* and Backward Castes (BCs) who are kicking, killing, burning, raping and destroying their little property. It is true that quarrel breaks out only between immediate neighbours. The Untouchables, who are at the bottom of the caste ladder, and the BCs are the immediate neighbours all over India. Since conflict is the core of caste system, it is natural that those at the top of the social hierarchy oppress those below them. But who gives the inspiration for the BCs to oppress the Untouchables? It is the inspiration and the philosophy behind it that is more important and not the actual action. The brain guides and the leg kicks. The leg kicks because the order came from the brain to kick. So who is the brain here? It is the Brahmin.

Nobody has analysed this situation better than Dr. B.R. Ambedkar:

> Historically Brahmins have been the most inveterate enemy of the servile classes (Shudras and the untouchable classes) who together constitute about 80% of the Hindu population.
>
> (Dr. Ambedkar: *What Congress and Gandhi Have Done to Untouchables*, Thacker & Co.,-1945 Bombay, p. 203).

That does not mean we can tolerate the Backward Caste violence on Untouchables. A majority of the BCs are as poor as the Untouchables. Just because they are "touchables" and the caste system has given "divine sanction" to it they are indulging in this violence. It is high time the Dravida Kazhagam warns the BC leaders that if they don't educate their fellow men against this violence, they will also suffer under Brahminism.

How to identify enemy

Dr. Ambedkar says the cardinal principles of Brahminism are six:

> (1) graded inequality between the different classes; (2) complete disarmament of the *shudras* and the untouchables; (3) complete prohibition of education of the *shudras* and the Untouchables; (4) ban on the *shudras* and the Untouchables occupying places of power and authority; (5) ban on the *shudras* and Untouchables acquiring property; (6) complete subjugation and suppression of women" (ibid). "Inequality is therefore the official doctrine of Brahminism" (ibid p.204).

Such of those Untouchables who think that BCs are their main enemy are wrong in their assessment. A true Ambedkarite knows how to identify his Enemy No.1. The BCs will go on kicking and killing the Untouchables as long as Brahminism continues to exist in India. So, leaders of Untouchables will have to educate their followers on how to identify the Enemy No.1. It is only after destroying this main enemy (principal contradiction), it will be possible to launch the attack on lesser evils. The landed castes and the BCs may have the political power and the muscle but have hardly any brain. Once you blast the brain, the next step of annihilating the brawn is a cakewalk.

Women libbers

India is the only country in the world where the Brahmins made education their exclusive monopoly. And also imposed strict penalty on learning by "low castes". The penalty included cutting the tongue and pouring molten lead into ears etc. Please read the *Manusmriti* (Asian Educational Services, C-2/15, SDA, New Delhi - 110 016, 1982) for more details.

If the vast majority of *shudras* and particularly the Untouchables today appear lifeless, spiritless, hopeless and thoroughly emasculated, it is because of this Brahmin law. Widows were burnt alive under a system of *sati*. But for Raja Rammohan Roy, this cruel system would have continued even to this day. Although *sati* is outlawed, we have even to this day some isolated cases of *sati*. And we have also any number of supporters for this cruel system. Widows are not allowed to re-marry. Women, not excluding Brahmin women, are the worst victims of this Brahmin law. So, women, particularly the Brahmin women, should consider the destruction of Brahminism their primary goal in life. It is only when Brahminism is dead true liberation of women can take place. Women libbers, please note.

If a "low caste" and particularly the Untouchable is a slave today, his wife is the slave of the slave. Who is responsible for this except the Brahmin philosophy?

Has there been any changes in the philosophy of Brahminism? No. Every Brahmin and his bum-lickers among non-Brahmins firmly believe in this philosophy of Brahminism even to this day. Mrs. Indira Gandhi is the greatest exponent of Brahminism. Her predecessor, Morarji Desai, was also the most ardent votary of Brahminism. I am yet to come across a Brahmin who has revolted against Brahminism, not excluding Jawaharlal Nehru. Brahmins in the marxist parties are no exception. The only exception was perhaps M.N. Roy. There may be some lesser known people like Prem Nath Bazaz, a Kashmiri Brahmin.

Intellect is nobody's monopoly

A fantastic theory is being propounded in Hindu India that Brahmins possess all the "merit" and that is why they happen to occupy all the important offices in India. Even our marxists believe in this theory. In West Bengal, in Jyoti Basu's marxist cabinet, there is not even a single Untouchable Cabinet Minister. The answer is that there is no "merited" MLA among Untouchables to be given the cabinet rank. This answer presupposes that the Untouchables and other "low castes" have no "merit" and Jyoti Basu's cabinet packed with Brahmins alone has all the "merit". It is based on this theory that Indira Gandhi's cabinet is also packed with over 50% Brahmins. So is the case in every state ministry, department or university, bank or educational institution. When this is brought to the notice of the Brahmins and their bum-lickers the usual answer that we get is that people are selected to posts on the basis of "merit" and Brahmins happened to be the "merited" people.

All right. Let us accept this theory. Yes. It is based on this theory that Brahmins have been ruling India ever since "independence". When the most brilliant and "merited" people are ruling, India should have been a paradise on earth. But what is the actual position? It is a beggar country. Its rank in the United Nations is 120. What is the rank of China? China has neither Brahmins nor gods. But China is within 20. How did such a thing happen? What is the use of this Brahmin "merit" which has no heart. "Merit" without heart is more dangerous. (V.T. Rajshekar: *Merit, My Foot*, Dalit Sahitya Akademy - 1996).

Who governs India?

The usual answer to this question is that the government is governing India.

This is not true. The government is not governing India. The government does not constitute the governing class. In India, what appears to the bare eyes as the "governing class" is not the truth. In India, neither the Prime Minister, President nor even the central cabinet constitute the governing class. They form only a portion of the governing class. Then who constitute the governing class? In India, the governing class comprise the top 10% of the Indian population — of this 5% are the Brahmins and the other five their bum-lickers. It is the Brahmin-Bania-feudal class. The "caste-class" octopus. In other words those subscribing to the philosophy of Brahminism constitute the governing class of India. To verify this, you have to go through the telephone directory of Delhi. You will know it yourself when you read the names. This is the position in all the cities. The governing class of India lives primarily in the metropolitan cities of India — Bombay, Delhi, Calcutta, Madras, Bangalore. It is a city-based elite.

This governing class is more powerful than the Central Government or the Prime Minister. If it says no, neither the PM, Central Cabinet or the State CM could do anything.

I will give you one most convincing example to prove the power of this "governing class" and how powerless is the Prime Minister and other paraphernalia. Untouchability is abolished not by law but in the Constitution itself and if anybody is seen observing it, he is punished with jail or fine or both. Observing untouchability is therefore, not merely an offence against law but an offence against the Constitution itself. But what happened? It is now how many years since the Constitution was launched - 1951? Did untouchability go? Do you doubt that Parliament. Prime Minister, Central Cabinet and the State Governments are insincere in their efforts to abolish untouchability? Why even Karunanidhi as Chief Minister of Tamil Nadu failed to abolish untouchability? Will he succeed, if he becomes the PM? Forget about all this. Could Periyar have succeeded if he had been made the PM? No. Neither the Constitution, the Government, Parliament, Supreme Court nor the State Governments can succeed in abolishing untouchability because the governing class of India wants untouchability to continue.

Who controls our brains?

If the ruling class wants anything, no power on earth can stop it. Come what may. So, the government is not "governing" India but it is the ruling class.

We can go on giving any number of examples but suffice it to say that in Hindu India the "Brahmin power" is superior to the

Constitution or the government. It is above everything else. Because Brahmins are the ruling class.

Marx, Lenin and even Mao were also well aware of this. When I was in China (1980) leading a goodwill delegation, many top Chinese leaders said they were aware of the influence of Brahmins in India. They called it the "Brahmin imperialism". Historians both Indian and foreign have admitted their centuries of supremacy as leaders of people, custodians of religion, unrivalled captains of every walk of life, owners of wealth and power besides being the trustees of the people's conscience as priests. Probably, no other class of people in the world ever possessed such an all-embracing power so exclusive as Brahmins. Indian culture is Brahmin culture. Our "glorious cultural heritage" is the achievements of Brahmins as the custodian of culture.

> *Devadhinam jagat sarvam*
> *Mantradhinam ta devata,*
> *Tan Mantram brahmanadhinam*
> *Brahmana mama devata.*

It means:

> The Universe is under the power of the gods; the gods are under the power of the *mantras*, the *mantras* are under the power of the Brahmins; therefore the Brahmins are our gods.
>
> (Abbe J.A. Dubois, *Hindu Manners, Customs and Ceremonies*, Oxford, Third Edition-1906, p.139).

Roots of fascism

If at all, there is anybody in Hindu India who knows that there is no god, it is the Brahmin priest, That is why, the Brahmins called themselves the "gods of earth (*Bhoodevatas*). And there are any number of bloody fools to believe it.

Whether it was during the Janata Party regime or during the Indira Gandhi rule, we have been witnessing a strong tendency towards dictatorship and fascism. When the Janata Party was in power we all knew the havoc played by the RSS, the

Brahmin-Bania organisation, which for the first time captured power in the Central Government. The RSS has been openly advocating upper caste dictatorship and did everything to impose a type of fascism. The same tendency was seen during the "Emergency" rule of Indira Gandhi and Sanjay Gandhi. It is because she tried to impose dictatorship, people are said to have voted her out and opted for Janata rule which outdid her in fascist tendencies. What we can make out from this is whether it is the Congress or the Janata, the tendency in Hindu India is towards fascist dictatorship. This is because Brahminism is the other name for fascism. In fact, the world's greatest fascists, Hitler, Mussolini etc. got their inspiration from Brahminism. The father of the fascist cult, Nietzche, who was the disciple of Schopenhauer, the grandfather of fascism, found consolation in the philosophy of *Upanishads*. The Brahmin philosophy based on the dangerous *karma* theory asks the poor to bear their poverty with a smiling face and resign to the fate.

Unquestioned obedience is what the fascist philosophy seeks. And the *Gita* (IV-39-40) preaches only such a philosophy:

> But the man of doubt, without knowledge and without faith, is lost; for him who is given to doubt there is neither this world nor that beyond, nor happiness.

The governing class tells the subjects to be detached and this detachment has proved to be a wonderful cover to be blind to the suffering of the poor.

The *karma* theory is a handy philosophy for the propertied class. Why the rich are rich? Because he did lots of *punya* (good deeds) in his previous birth. Why the poor are poor? Because he committed lots of sins. Will he be able to acquire *punya*, if he serves the god? Yes, let us see. Let him serve without putting any conditions. If he is doing any good deed, he has to do it without any preconditions. Without expecting any result. If he expects any result and therefore does good deeds, he may not get the result.

Can we ever think of a more convenient philosophy than the *karma* theory in the hands of this ruling class? The caste system gives the divine sanction to the *karma* theory. Hindu god Krishna tells us in the *Gita* that he is the author of the caste system (*Gita* 4-13, 10-36-41). The Upanishads have also sanctioned the caste system:

> "... those who are of pleasant conduct here - the prospect is, indeed, they will enter a pleasant womb, either the bomb of a Vaishya. But those who are of stinking conduct here - the prospect is, indeed, that they will enter a stinking womb, either the womb of a dog or the bomb of a swine or the womb of an outcaste" (*Chandogya Upanishad* 5-10-7).

What is the duty of the *shudra*? The *Gita* (18-44) says: "Service is the duty of shudra". The Laws of the Manu (1.91) says "the lord prescribed the *shudra*, to serve meekly ever these three (other) castes". "The king himself must order the *shudra* to serve the twice-born castes (Manu 8-410). To serve Brahmins is the highest duty of the shudra.

Why Brahmins praise Gandhi?

There cannot be a greater anti-socialist if not anti-human philosophy than Brahminism. Gandhi, the great Hindu leader, upheld this Brahmin philosophy and that is why although it was one RSS Brahmin who killed Gandhi, it is the Brahmins who today are the biggest votaries of gandhism. Brahminism glorifies sacrifice and suffering as a great virtue. Nietzche's philosophy bears close resemblance to Brahminism and particularly borrows a lot from the *karma* theory. It is the god that wants people to be unequal. So there is a divine sanction. Gandhi justified it creating his dangerous theory of trusteeship.

"The philosophy of fascism was inspired by the Aryan spirit of caste system..." (M.N. Roy, *Fascism* p.40). "The philosophy of fascism is essentially identical with Indian spiritualism" (p. 43). The *Gita, Upanishads* are the Bible of fascism. What was the aim of fascism? To destroy marxism. What is the goal of Brahminism? To maintain the *Varnashrama Dharma* and the privileges of the upper castes. Brahminism is, therefore, the father of fascism. Adolf Hitler, and his fascist hordes fomented and launched an artificial hatred of Jews in Germany. And in India, Brahminism is preaching a similar artificial hatred of Muslims and asking Hindus to drive them out of India, drink their blood. The anti-Muslim hatred of RSS is nothing but another version of the ferocious anti-semitism of nazis.

Saner elements of the whole world joined hands and destroyed nazism in the battlefield of the Second World War. The child may be dead. But the father of fascism is yet to be killed. If India has to be saved from fascism, we have to destroy Brahminism.

Therefore, such "Anti-Brahmin domination conferences" should be held all over India,. And the Dravida Kazhagam will have to take the initiative.

II - Sacred Scriptures: A Bundle of Contradictions

Those who have critically gone through the Brahmin Sacred Scriptures particularly the *Upanishads* and the *Gita* would have found how it is repetitive, word-mongering and packed with speculative philosophy. The description of the *Atman* and *Brahman* is typically wordy and repetitive (*Brahmavidyopanishad* 81-111), (*Tejo-Bindupanishad* III-1-43), (*Anna-Punopanishad* II-3-6), (*Darshanopanishad* X-1-5).

Those who have nothing to convey always say it with a forest of words. Brevity is the soul of rationalism. But if the intention is to mystify and not to specify then you have to be verbose. The Sacred Scriptures (in Sanskrit translated to English by Max Mueller) are intended more to mystify the people than to convince them of any rational argument. Meaningless words are woven into a cobweb to see that the reader is confined, caught, confused and cribbed. The whole thing looks so absurd, just a jungle of words without any meaning or significance.

After all, the world of facts enlivens the world of words. Even the most eloquent oration, stentorian voice, though a fascinating music to the ears, proves futile if divorced from the facts of life.

> The wisest in council, the ablest in debate and the most agreeable companion in the commerce of human life, is that man who has assimilated to his understanding the greatest number of facts. (J. Landis, as quoted by Justice V.R. Krishna Iyer of the Supreme Court in his judgment of Nov.14, 1980).

Tejo-Bindupanishad (III-48-59) says that everything is false:

> "The form of the mind is false... All the Veda is always false. Know that all the Shastra is false... Know all living creature to be false, all enjoyment to be false... know that all grief and delight are false.... victory and defeat are all false....".

So everything is false, according to *Tejo-Bindupanishad.* If everything is false as per the *Upanishad* why the Brahmin priests, who parrot-like recite the Sacred Scriptures, do not refuse to take money which also must be false? In the same *Upanishad* (V-31-58) even the study of the Vedas is declared false. Then why the Brahmins give so much value to the Vedas? Can there be a bigger contradiction?

Another fantastic thing is that one Brahmin god does not like another Brahmin god. The sectarian *Upanishads* proclaim their gods as superior to the other. The beauty of the Brahmin philosophy is that one Brahmin god hates the other god. It is amazing that these gods behave worse than we ordinary mortals specially when they fight between themselves.

Sharabhopanishad (17-19) claims Vishnu a devotee of Shiva. If god is one and the only one in several names and forms and if he is indivisible, as the Brahmin interpreters of these Sacred Scriptures are never tired of saying, why this rival claims and conflicting salesmanship to push their favourite gods? *Sharabhopanishad* claims "Lord Shankara, the foremost of all gods". If god is one, how could there be a ranking? What nonsense. And they call it Sacred Scriptures and we bloody fools believe it.

Max Mueller verdict

See the judgement passed by one of the greatest authorities of all times on the Sacred Scriptures. Prof. Max Mueller, a great German Sanskrit scholar, commenting on the *Brahmanas* says:

> No one would have supposed that at so early a period and in so primitive a state of society, there could have risen up a literature which for pedantry and downright absurdity can hardly be matched anywhere... The general character of these works is marked by shallow and insipid grand eloquence, by priestly conceit, and antiquarian pedantry. It is most important to the historian that he should know how soon the fresh and healthy growth of a nation can be blighted by priestcraft and superstition. It is most important he should know

that nations are liable to these epidemics in their youth as well as in their dotage. These works deserve to be studied as the physician studies the twaddle of idiots, and the raving of madmen. (*Ancient Sanskrit Literature*, Panini edition p.200).

In *Prashnopanishad* (II-16-23) complete abstinence from contact with women including the wife is prescribed to reach the state of mind of becoming the *Brahmana*. But in *Yogashikhopanishad* (I-52-8) sex is strictly recommended to become *Brahman*. The Sacred Scriptures are so full of contradictions that sometime not only one scripture vetoes the other but in the same scripture the second para contradicts the first and goes on like that.

Humbug & hypocrisy

Brahminism is more a law than a religion like Islam or Christianity. It is full of rules, regulations, dos and don'ts and formalities with no content of moral fibre. It is humbug and hypocrisy personified. Brahminism is satisfied merely with formality. Any sin or crime can be committed but the *Upanishads* are capable of washing it off. *Bhasmajabalopanishad* II says: "He who makes use of this (*Bhasma*) is purified from the sin of slaughtering his mother" and *Sharbopanishad* (35-39) says those studying *shastra* "is hallowed from the sin of sharing the bed with his guru's wife."

In all Brahmin temples, at the very entrance a big board is displayed listing the different charges to wash off your sins. Any sin can be removed by paying appropriate amount to the priest.

The *Bhagwad Gita* (IV-48-53-54) says there is no need for knowledge or even the study of the Vedas. Even the worst skunk will get the god's blessings provided he has the faith. That means there is no respect for scholarship or devotion but only faith — unquestioned faith, blind faith. No need for inquiry, no need for reasoning. What a fantastic theory.

Upanishads declare the world to be unreal. If the world is not

> there at all, if neither the doer nor the object of the deed is at all existent, then where is the question of performing duties, of doing deeds? (Arun Shourie, *Hinduism: Essence & Consequences*, Vikas-1979 p.168).

Whenever we criticise Brahminism for not calling upon people to work, not to speak of socially relevant work, the defenders of Brahminism quote the Upanishads asking the people to work. But what do they mean by this "work"? When someone urges us to "work" today we are apt almost automatically to assume that he is asking us to engage in struggles in the real world, to engage in deeds with our fellow-men. But this is not the meaning that would have come to the minds of the authors of the Upanishads, the *Brahma-Sutras* etc. For them, their readers and listeners, "work" meant the rituals, sacrifices etc. prescribed in the *Purva-Mimansa*, the chants glorified in the *Sama Veda* or the *Chandogyopanishad*, they meant the recitation of Vedas, sacrifices, gifts, penance, fasting as the *Brihad-Aryakopanishad* (4-4-22) refers to them (Arun Shourie ibid p.179).

Contradictions is the essence of the Sacred Scriptures. Anybody can interpret it in any way he likes. And Shankara, Ramanuja, Madhwa, Gandhi, Tilak, Radhakrishnan and even Godse have interpreted it as they liked and the debate has been going on for centuries. The beauty is that both the saint and the devil can quote from the same scripture to justify his words and deeds. The so-called flexibility of the scriptures is, therefore, not accidental but deliberate.

Ethics & social responsibility

The Sacred Scriptures manufactured by the Brahmins try to paint a mischievous picture which is intended to confuse the viewer from whichever angle he looks. The intention, therefore, is clear: to confuse, confound, overawe and misguide the people and thereby the Brahmins are helped to run away with the loot. The Brahmins have successfully played this hoax on the gullible people by declaring everything to be *mithya* (unreal).

Arun Shourie ,who himself later joined the Hindu nazi party and became a Union Cabinet Minister, says:

> For the basic question is as follows: if man is declared to be an indescribable non-corporality, if all empirical relationships are declared to be chimerical, if the empirical world itself is declared to be non-existent, then where is the place for ethics, where is the scope for urging us to look at and help alleviate the privations of our fellowmen? What, as Schweitzer once asked, has ethics to do in an unreal world? Where is the question of social responsibility in a society that doesn't even exist? (Arun Shourie Ibid. p. 211).

The *Gita*(XVI-1-5) speaks of compassion to creatures, but why no reference to compassion to humans? Nor is there any reference to exploitation of man by man. In Christianity, Islam or any other religion there is some ethics attached to the religion. But under Brahminism there is none. It is very easy to wash off the sins — just recite the *mantra* or wear a *mala* (beads) or apply *vibhuti* (ash) or offer some money or some such thing. When it is so easy to wash off the sins, why not commit more and more sins and then wash it off by chanting a *mantra*? It is all funny, ridiculous.

That is why our advice to all those critics of Brahmins and their scriptures is not to argue and write "scholarly" articles criticising their scriptures. There is no point in criticising them because if you pinpoint one mistake, the Brahmins can defend that "mistake" by quoting from another scripture. Since the brahminical scriptures are a bundle of contradictions, the Brahmins can defend any crime of theirs. Then why go to argue with them?

Commenting on what Krishna tells Arjuna (*Gita* 18,17):

> He who is free from egotistic notions, whose mind is not tainted though he kills these creatures, he kills not, he is not bound".

Commenting on this, Arun Shourie says:

> This is also the reason on account of which Krishna himself, for all his amorous adventures, is declared by the *Upanishads* to have been a celibate. (Ibid p.220).

Argument is tailor-made to the needs of the situation. Krishna's sex acts, if it had been committed by anybody else, would have been dubbed as the most lecherous acts on earth. But why the same actions are justified in the case of Krishna? What fantastic double-standards these scriptures preach. If Krishna does it, it is divine. If others do it, he is a fornicator. (Dr. B.R. Ambedkar: *Riddle of Rama & Krishna*, Dalit Sahitya Akademy, 1995).

Never argue with a Brahmin because he employs neither logic, reasoning, scientific proof nor rational argument. Brahminical scriptures are the cause of the Brahmin's perverted thinking.

We can quote a dozen *Upanishads* which can give a dozen meanings to the same text, same word, like *Om*. It is only when different interpretations and meanings are given, it is possible to fool the gullible. Quote any passage, give any interpretation or meaning you like and still you can get away with it. If anybody challenges it, dub him anti-god, anti-Brahmin, anti-Hindu and finish him. Those who are considered to be the greatest commentators on the Sacred Scriptures like Shankara have kept quiet on this bundle of contradictions in the Sacred Scriptures. Anybody taking up the study of scriptures seriously from a scientific angle will indeed go mad. Any meaning can be given to any word or any sentence. *Upanishads, Brahmasutras, Gita* make diametrically contradictory assertions. Shankara gives one meaning but Ramanuja differs with it. In the most important issue of what is *Atman* and what is *Brahman* different *Upanishads* give different and often contradictory meanings. The two top commentators, Shankara and Ramanuja, make the confusion worse confounded. It is all a farce. Arun Shourie, a Punjabi Brahmin, has written one whole book to prove this point.

Wolf & lamb

Brahminism is said to be preaching *Sarve jana sukhino bhavantu* meaning anybody and everybody will be protected. That means both the exploiter and the exploited can co-exist. Is this possible? Can the wolf and the lamb co-exist? How can antagonistic forces with diametrically opposite interests co-exist? The wolf may go on assuring that it will look after the lamb but how long? When it is hungry, it will eat off the lamb. This is what happens under the law of Brahminism. *Sarve jana sukhino bhavantu* is the most convenient philosophy to hand over the lamb to the wolf on a silver platter. The poor, innocent lamb went on believing in Brahminism for centuries and became its victim. Can there be a more heartless philosophy in the world?

Brahmins from centuries constituted India's only leisured class. Since every "learned profession" was "reserved" for them by themselves, naturally they could master only three arts: reading, writing and speaking. They knew nothing else. All professions connected with these three arts were "reserved" for them. They were never producers of wealth. Because, to produce wealth one has to work and to work one has to sweat but "working" is prohibited. Nor was there any need to work because work was "reserved" for the servile class who were too willing to do it.

When the Brahmins were prohibited from working but got plenty to eat and plenty of time to sleep, what else they can do? So the idle mind naturally becomes the devil's workshop. They started concocting things so that the status quo prevailed. The Sacred Scriptures are their most ingenious inventions to befool the masses to retain the position, privileges and properties that were made the exclusive preserve of the Brahmins. They got themselves busy with the study of Sacred Scriptures and their interpretations. As they had plenty of time to waste it was a pastime with them to stuff empty boxes. When different meanings and interpretations failed they started indulging in repetitions. Even when such blatantly fake and meaningless efforts became apparent to many curious eyes, look at the reverence with which the gullible *shudras* hold these Sacred Scriptures. What bloody fools they must be.

The sole aim is to establish the supremacy of the Brahmin. The thief became not only the police and the prosecutor but also the judge, jailor and the hangman — all combined in one. Is there any philosophy in the world parallel to this?

World's cruelest social system

Perhaps the Hindu India presents the world's cruelest social system imposed on the natives by the alien Brahmins. Here the society is so systematically segmented that foreign scholars will be simply baffled by its complex nature. Every section of the population is literally bludgeoned to enforce obedience to the Brahmin who is declared as the *Bhoodevata* (god on earth). Not only each section is assigned a place in the caste pyramid but even the food each segment has to eat, the dress they have to wear, the language they have speak are all decided by the Brahmin. There are any number of restrictions on feeding and social intercourse. Brahmins decided who and what is polluting and what is sacred. The Hindu caste system (*Chatur Varna*), a cunning invention of the Brahmin to enforce his superiority, is a wonder of the world. Each caste and subcaste has its own civil and religious disabilities and privileges. The entire edifice of caste, with an ascending scale of reference and descending degree of contempt, is designed by the Brahmin to maintain his over-lordship.

After giving the above description of the caste system in his famous book, *Caste & Race in India*, (Popular Prakashan, 1999), G.S. Ghurye, himself a Brahmin and considered a top social scientist, was honest enough to castigate his own *jatwalas* (castemen) in the following words.

> A Brahmin never bows to anyone who is not a Brahmin, but requires others to salute him; and when he is saluted by a member of a non-Brahmin caste he only pronounces a benediction. Some of the lower castes carry their reverence for the Brahmins, especially in Northern India, to such extremes that they will not cross the shadow of a Brahmin, and sometimes will not take their food without sipping water in which the big toe of a Brahmin is dipped. The Brahmin, on the other hand, is so conscious of his superiority that he does not condescend to bow even to the idols of gods in a Shudra's house. The Brahmin has been regarded as the most important subject, needing protection from the king, so much so that the king is styled the protector of the Brahmins and the cows, other subjects being regarded as too insignificant to be mentioned. (p. 14-15).
>
> Brahmins were exempted from capital punishment, and when confined in forts, they were more liberally treated than the other classes. (Ibid p. 15).
>
> The effect of these rules was that the priestly profession was entirely monopolized by the Brahmins, leaving aside the ministrants of the aboriginal deities, while they were seen plying any trade or calling which suited their tastes and which was not polluting. (Ibid p.16).

Under Brahminism anything is possible provided it is advantageous to the Brahmin. The Satya Sai Baba "creating something out of nothing" is based on this Brahmin principle because he is god himself. The Brahmin can create without material because the "god" can create without material. This is based on the theory that the Brahmin has the power to accomplish whatever he wants without material. What logic.

Mad, mad world

> The scriptures, we are told, are unquestionable because they emanate from Brahmin. But how do we know that they emanate from the Brahmin? From the fact that scriptures themselves tell us that He is their source... Brahman is omniscient because scriptures emanate from Him and the scriptures are valid because they have emanated from an omniscient being. We know Brahmin to be omniscient because the scriptures say He is omniscient and we know the scriptures to be a valid

> means of knowledge because they have emanated from the omniscient one. (Arun Shourie, Ibid p.288).

What fantastic arguments. Only Brahmins are capable of it.

It is because of this reason Brahminism could withstand the multitude of attacks on it including the mightiest attack of Budhism. Brahminism could survive all the earthquakes because anybody can pick up from the Sacred Scriptures a passage or two to justify anything. You can find a passage to propagate socialism and at the same time to defend exploitation. You can find a sentence or two preaching against sex and also in favour of sex. You can be a supporter of both liberation of women as well as subjugation of women. You can make money stooping to any means and yet defend it through a passage in the scripture. At the same time somebody else might denounce such rapacious acquisition of wealth. Scriptures are a bottomless pit, a boneless wonder, you can twist it to any shape, any size. You can give it any colour. A mad, mad world.

India's most corrupt Prime Minister

P.V. Narasimha Rao, an Andhra Brahmin, who come to be called as India's most corrupt Prime Minister, was not denounced even by a single Shankaracharya because no Brahmin can be corrupt as per the Sacred Scriptures. So too Jayalalita, a Brahmin, who thrice became Chief Minister of Tamil Nadu and amassed hundreds of crores of rupees.

Why the sacred scriptures are capable of such contradictory interpretations? Are the Brahmins bloody fools to indulge in such nonsense? No, there is a method in their madness.

> Contrary propositions were affirmed and retained because contrary propositions were needed... And this is one reason why contrary assertions find a place in the corpus. To dwarf man, to convince him that he is puny in the face of the order of things, we have to create and magnify a lord, we have to maintain that He is the only creative agent, that alone is the author of every thing. (Arun Shourie, Ibid. p.339).

Hindus can hardly think

That is why the Hindus can hardly think. And if anybody can think among Hindus he can hardly think straight. Many of them are downright perverts. The tendency in India is to split and not to unite and consolidate. Why every party or organisation gets divided? Why clashes and conflicts are so common in India? Why Hindus cannot work as a single cohesive nation? Why do they always divide and sub-divide? Why they spend so much of time quarreling with each other?

Brahminism is the sole cause for all our crisis. India was never a nation and can never be a nation. Unity is not in our blood. Every foreign invasion took place at the invitation of a Hindu ruler. This is a fact of history which was admitted by Guru Golwalkar himself in his book *Bunch of Thoughs* (Vikram Prakashana-1968 p. 205). Because Brahminism tells us to have double-standards, double-dealing and double-thinking. Even double-crossing. That is why Hindus are basically dishonest compared to Christians or Muslims. Exceptions prove the rule.

That is why a Hindu can never think straight. Nay, it is those who think straight that are laughed at, despised and finally hunted down like a mad dog. No Hindu will show mercy on another who departs from the conventional beaten track. Dissent is dangerous under Brahminism. That is why Brahmins in particular and Hindus in general have hardly produced any revolutionary. That is why Hindu India is not having a revolution. Every act of a Hindu is the result of his deep saturation in the philosophy of Brahminism, its conflicting and contradictory approaches and confusing conflicts.

The *Brahma Sutras* rejected the Jain view of soul on the ground that it suffered from contradictions. But the Brahmin view cannot be rejected even if there are any number of contradictions. Why? Because the Brahmin is always right. Who says he is right? It is the Brahmin - the Gods of Earth. Those who doubt this and those who question this are laughed at and if he still persists in questioning the Brahmin, he will be finished.

> But what annoys one is the intolerance of the Brahmin scholar towards any attempt to expose the Brahminic literature. He himself would not play the part of an iconoclast even where it is necessary. And he would not allow such non-Brahmins as have the capacity to do so to play it. If any non-Brahmin were to make an attempt the Brahmin scholars would engage in a conspiracy of silence, take no notice of him, condemn him outright on some flimsy grounds or dub his work useless. As a writer engaged in the exposition of the Brahmanic literature, I have been a victim of such mean tricks.
>
> (Dr. Ambedkar, *The Untouchables*, Bharatiya Bauddha Shiksha Parishad, Shravasti-1988, p. xii Rs. 12).
>
> (The entire works of Dr. Ambedkar have been since reprinted by the Maharashtra Government as *Writings & Speeches of Dr. Babasaheb Ambedkar*).

Mahopanishad (II-74-77) described those who doubt as dirt. Liberation is reserved only for those who suspend doubt. *Maitreyopanishad* (2-17) also lays stress on faith and condemns those who question the scriptures and predicts the destruction of the doubters.

There is no change in the thinking of Brahmins even in the 21st century. Brahminism does not believe in change because it is *Sanatana Dharma*, never changing.

The Guru cult

After saying all this the Brahmin introduces a unique institution to perpetuate the Brahmin hegemony — the *Guru* cult. Brahminism says none can master the scriptures unless he is initiated into by a *guru* (teacher) and such a *guru* must be none other than the Brahmin. Please note such a *guru* is above the god. Nobody has the right to study the scriptures on his own without the help of the *guru*. And this *guru*, we are told, is god incarnate.

This *guru* may be a fraud, fornicator, thug, drunkard, cheat, murderer, characterless, idiot. Does not matter. India is full of such *gurus* today. Satya Sai Baba is charged with murdering six people in his own bedroom but right from the President and Prime Minister downwards all VVIPs make a beeline to his place and fall on his feet. No arm of law dare touch him. Chandraswamy is another famous case. We have thousands of such scoundrels but they all command respect because they belong to the category of *guru*.

Marathi Brahmin saint

The *shastras* do not permit a Hindu to appoint any one of his liking to be his *guru* even if he is well-versed in the Sacred Scriptures and recite it by heart. This is made clear by many Brahmin saints like Ramadas who is alleged by the RSS to have inspired Shivaji to establish a Hindu Raj. Dr. Ambedkar (*Annihilation of Caste*) refers to Ramadas' book in which this Marathi Brahmin saint has clearly ruled out accepting an Untouchable as *guru* even if he is a learned Sanskrit pundit. The office of the *guru* is therefore well-protected. It is not the learning that makes a *guru*, but his *jati* (caste).

The institution of the *guru* is invented with the object of perpetuating the Brahmin hegemony. The continuity of the Brahmin imperialism is ensured by this unique institution. And every precaution is taken to see that this institution is never exposed to any danger. The *guru* is strictly warned not to talk to an atheist, a rationalist, or a non-believer. Never ague with anybody who questions the supremacy of Brahminism but finish him. No mercy on dissenters. Look at the abuse heaped on Charvaka.

> Hence does the doctrine perpetuate itself, hence does it put itself beyond the reach of rational questioning, hence does it ensure that only those who have already suspended doubt will receive it, hence does it ensure that those who receive it will swallow it whole. (Arun Shourie, Ibid p.359).

It must be clear by now that Hindus can never be rational and straight. Brahminism and rationalism can never go together. "A person can either be a Hindu or Communist. He cannot be both". (M.S. Golwalkar, *Bunch of Thoughts* p.53).

And yet Brahminism is called the "most tolerant religion in the world" —protecting everybody under its umbrella. Can there be a bigger lie than this? Brahminism is tolerant only to the extent that it gives scope for diverse interpretations but those who question the basis of its philosophy is mercilessly put down. See the fate of the Budha, Basavanna, Guru Nanak, Raja Rammohan Roy, Narayana Guru, Dr. Ambedkar.

> In the *Ramayana*, Rama is made to say that the Buddha is a thief, the Thatagata is *nastik* or an atheist. A wise man who can help should therefore not be inclined towards *nastika*. (C.V. Vaidya, *Epic India* p.377).

Even M.K. Gandhi was killed by a Brahmin. How many attempts were made on the life of Dr. Ambedkar and Periyar? How can such a society be called tolerant?

Mad dogs of orthodoxy

The following verdict given by Dr. B.R. Ambedkar, India's greatest intellectual and an authority on the subject on Brahmins, Brahminism and their Hinduism, is worth quoting:

> The only thing I did not know was how the meek and non-violent-looking Hindu can be violent when anybody attacks his Sacred Books. I became aware of it as never before when last year I received a shower of letters from angry Hindus, who became quite unbalanced by my speech on the subject delivered in Madras. The letters were full of filthy abuse, unmentionable and unprintable, and full of dire threats to my life. Last time they treated me as a first offender and let me off with mere threats. I don't know what they will do this time. For on reading this book they are sure to find more cause for anger at what in their eyes is a repetition of the offence in an aggravated form for having brought forth chapter and verse to show that what goes by the name of Sacred Books contain fabrications which are political in their motive, partisan in their composition and fraudulent in their purpose. I do not propose to take any notice of their vilifications or their threats. For I know

> that they are a base crew who, professing to defend their religion, have made religion a matter of trade. They are more selfish than any other set of beings in the world, and are prostituting their intelligence to support the vested interests of their class. It is a matter of no small surprise that when the mad dogs of orthodoxy are let loose against a person who has the courage to raise his voice against the so-called Sacred Books of the Hindus, eminent Hindus occupying lofty places, claiming themselves to be highly educated and who could be expected to have no interest and have a free and open mind become partisans, join the outcry. Even Hindu Judges of High Courts and Hindu Prime Ministers of Indian states do not hesitate to join their kind. They go further. They not only lead the howl against him but even join in the hunt. What is outrageous is that they do so because they believe that their high stations in life would invest their words with an amount of terror which would be sufficient enough to cow down any and every opponent of orthodoxy. What I would like to tell these amiable gentlemen is that they will not be able to stop me by their imprecations. They do not seem to be aware of the profound and telling words of Dr. Johnson who when confronted with an analogous situation said: "I am not going to be deterred from catching a cheat by the menaces of a ruffian". I do not wish to be rude to these high-placed critics, much less do I want to say that they are playing the part of a ruffian interested in the escape of a cheat. But I do want to tell them two things; firstly that I propose, no matter what happens, to follow the determination of Dr. Johnson in the pursuit of historical truth by the exposure of the Sacred Books so that the Hindus may know that it is the doctrines contained in their Sacred Books which are responsible for the decline and fall of their country and their society; secondly, if the Hindus of this generation do not take notice of what I have to say I am sure the future generation will. I do not despair of success. For I take consolation in the words of poet Bhavabhuti who said: "Time is infinite and earth is vast, some day there will be born a man who will appreciate what I have said".
>
> (Dr. Ambedkar, *Who Are the Shudras,* Thackers-1970 p xvii - xviii).

Can these mad dogs of orthodoxy be called tolerant at any time? How can a social system that subjects a vast majority of its members to unparalleled barbarity be called tolerant? How can a set of people who describe the dissenters as demonic be called tolerant? How can a ruling class that sent the Army, which is universally used only against external enemies, to enter the Sikhs' holiest shrine, Golden Temple, at Amritsar and killed thousands of Sikhs —men, women and children — who were praying inside in the infamous "Blue Star Operation" (1984), be called practitioners of non-violence?

The Muslim, Christian and Sikh societies are today facing all the state-sponsored Hindu war and violence because all these three egalitarian religions are "threatening" the brahminical values.

Collective salvation

To counter these charges the Brahmins instantly produce some show-pieces — a company Negro — such *shudras* who have attained the highest places in life. How could they reach such a pinnacle of glory had it not been for the "tolerance" of Hinduism, we are asked. Come on, who are these *shudras* who achieved the brahminhood: Swami Vivekananda, Satya Sai Baba, Swami Chinmayananda. There are any number of such show pieces. If you examine them carefully, we will find them more loyal than their masters.

> Moreover, the individual *shudra* who attained the status of honour in the records of the doctrine was one who had internalised the notions of the doctrine, one who had, in fact, become a Brahmin in his very psyche. What these exceptions testify to, then, is not tolerance but co-option, what we are seeing at work is not a society tolerating those who oppose it but a society that is co-opting the ring-leaders of those who might oppose it. (Arun Shourie Ibid. p.363).

This is called the "individual salvation". By imitating a Brahmin, a *shudra* or *ati-shudra* can go up the ladder. But no "collective salvation" is tolerated.

Sanskritisation, westernisation, industrialisation and lately globalisation have only helped to strengthen Brahminism. These new recruits to Brahminism have given an outer cover to the Brahmin skin. These neo-Brahmins are more dangerous than the Brahmins. The latest to strengthen the Brahmin fortress is the Indian brand of marxism and nobody has helped defend Brahminism better than our marxists. In fact they out-do the most orthodox Brahmins in their loyalty to Brahminism. Marxist Brahmins have proved to be more dangerous than the RSS Brahmins. (V.T. Rajshekar: *How Marx Failed in Hindu India*, DSA-1988).

This has been the state of affairs in India from the very beginning, ever since Brahminism devoured Budhism — the greatest liberating humanist philosophy. As the Brahmins occupying the apex of the caste pyramid had everything under their control they never had any problems to face and the leisure that was available to them in plenty was used for speculation. The idle brain became the devil's workshop and produced a jungle of Sacred Scriptures which caused all our misery and reduced India to a beggar nation. How beautiful it is when the entire nation pledges its brain to the safe custody of the Brahmins. What more does a ruling class want when its subjects delegate them the power to think?

Hindu India has become a vast intellectual wasteland. Nobody gets angry in this *Dharma Bhoomi*, its sacred soil, because their brains are safe with Brahmins. India has become the sick man of the world because of this essential Hindu trait of unquestioned obedience to authority. And parrot-like we repeat to uphold this "glorious cultural heritage" of India.

Brahminism is the sole cause of our degradation. India under Brahmin imperialism was in the Third World. But while other nations managed to at least inch forward, India sank deeper and deeper. And so much so India today slipped from the Third World to the Fourth World. Three cheers to Brahminism.

III - Max Muller's Contribution to Promote Aryan Racism

Nobody has contributed so much to the glorification of the Aryan myth as much as Friedrich Max Muller, the great German Indologist, Professor of Comparative Philosophy and Fellow of the All Souls at Oxford. In a lecture in 1861, he said :

> "the first ancestors of Indians, Persians, the Greeks, the Romans, the Slavs, the Celts and the Germans were (once) living together within the same enclosure, nay under the same roof". (Muller F.M.: *Lectures on the Science of Language*, London, 1862 p.213).

He produced the "evidence" for this from the *Rig Veda* which he described as the "oldest book then known to scholars". Nobody has done greater service to the Aryan Brahmins of India as much as Max Muller. But for Max Muller all their (Sanskrit) scriptures would have been forgotten and dead. Because, it was this German Indologist who for the first time translated into English the entire text running into hundreds of pages calling it the *Sacred Books of the East*.

Nirad Chaudhury on Max Muller

These Sacred Scriptures were never in the written form. The Brahmins were against writing down their scriptures as it was against their religious tradition. These texts were memorised and passed from generation to generation through the word of mouth. So much so, it would have been forgotten and dead long back but for Max Muller. So much is the service rendered by this great German scholar for whom the Brahmins should have remained grateful. As gratefulness is never a part of the Aryan vocabulary, they vehemently criticised Max Muller as a Christian missionary with the selfish motive of converting India into a Christian territory. (Nirad C. Chaudhury: *Scholar Extraordinary*, Orient Paperbacks, Delhi, 1974).

That Max Muller did a thankless job will be evident to all those who read the above book of Nirad Babu. All those who feed milk to the serpent will get bitten some time or other. The serpent may drink the milk and yet bite. This is what the Aryans did to Max Muller whom Nirad described as a "world figure", "a legend". Max Mueller raised Sanskrit to such a pre-eminent level and called it the "storehouse of world knowledge", "mother of all languages". Alas, such a language has been deliberately destroyed by the very creators of this language, the Brahmins.

Christian ethos

Not only they destroyed their own language but took to English which as of today is called the only "national language" of India.

If Hindi is the "national language" as the Aryan rulers of India sometime claim, why the largest circulated Hindi daily of India, *Nav BharatTimes*, is not called a "national daily?" Why only English dailies like the *Times of India, Indian Express, Statesman* etc. are called "national dailies"? This is because they are in English and have all-India circulation. Hence the very Aryan propagators of Sanskrit admit English as the national language.

The problem with Max Muller was that he never visited India and without having a personal experience of the actual social, moral and religious life of the Aryans he praised them to the skies. As a Christian, brought up under Christian ethos, he viewed the Aryans who neither had an ethos nor believed in any value system. He never knew the stark exploitative life led by the Aryans.

However, the Aryans, experts in the game of exploitation, exploited Max Muller to the fullest extent and finally threw him out sucking him dry. They used the Aryan race theory to befriend the British and bagged important positions in the British administration, educational and business field to further exploit the indigenous people of India.

Muller called a racist

Some European scholars who called Max Muller a racist are not far wrong. By his Aryan race theory he only whetted the racist appetite of Aryans who made full use of his theory: (i) to gain favour of the British and ride roughshod over the non-Aryan majority Indians; (ii) the Aryan race theory also helped the White Western British, French, Portuguese rulers who came to India to spread their Christian faith among Aryans; (iii) many upper castes/Aryans/Hindus got converted to Christianity to gain favour from the European rulers.

The Aryan racist theory thus played havoc with India and Indians. But the upper castes/Aryans took to Christianity not because they liked Christianity but with a selfish motive.

India's divided church

It is this conversion of upper castes, mainly Brahmins, to Christianity which created two rival churches in India. Over 80% of the Christian population is Dalit and these Dalit Christians are ruled by the upper caste Christians who control the church. (V.T. Rajshekar: *Christians & Dalit Liberation*, Dalit Sahitya Akademy, 2000).

It was only at the fag end of his life Muller came to the conclusion that Aryanism/Brahminism/Hinduism cannot be reformed and hence he advocated conversion of Hindus to Christianity (Nirad Chaudhury, Ibid p.33).

But the moment he started thinking on these lines the Aryans thought this was the right time to disown him after making full use of his Aryan race theory.

It is a pity that Max Muller never made a study of the "Hindu mind". (V.T. Rajshekar: *Know the Hindu Mind*, DSA-1990).

The Aryan Brahmins will never be anything other than Brahmins. Even if they get converted to Christianity they will continue to practice their racism inside the church. This is what they are doing as Syrian Christians, Goan Christians and Manglorean Christians.

Muller heart-broken

Max Muller died (Oct.28, 1900) a disappointed man, heart-broken.

Muller said Aryans brought both cult and culture to Europe. He described a visit to Britain by Raja Ram Mohan Roy, founder of the Brahmo Samaj, in unmistakably Aryan terms, as an attempt to join hands and to complete the world-wide circuit.... (Muller F.M.: *Biographical Essays*, 1884, p.9).

Such mutual admiration continued and both the British and the Aryans exploited the Aryan myth to their advantage. Together, the two exploited the indigenous peoples of India who today constitute over 85% of the country's population.

Here is a quotation from an authority on Muller's writings. He insisted that "what has taken place since the commencement of the British Government in India is only a reunion... of the members of the same great family". (Wilson, J: *India Three Thousand Years Ago*, Bombay, 1858, p.42).

Muller debunked

The British scholar, Martin Maw, in his Licester University doctorate thesis published as a book titled, *Visions of India* (Vertag Peter Lang 1990), debunks and destroys Muller's Aryan race theory. Says Martin Maw:

> Though Muller's "work has been devalued or altogether discredited, modern scholars have shown little hesitation in acknowledging Friedrich Max Muller as the founding father of the science of comparative religion" (p. 19).

Muller did the thankless job of translating the *Rig Veda* without ever visiting India, without ever understanding that it is the *Purusha Sukta* part of this most important of the Vedas that preaches and propagates the obnoxious caste system which for the first time in the history of humankind invents the theory of racism. Poor Muller also translated and edited the 54-volume collection called the *Sacred Books of the East*. His book, *My Autobiography: A Fragment*, was published posthumously in 1901.

Muller inspired a good lot of European scholars on the Aryan race theory. Sir William Jones, a noted English jurist, compared the *Vedanta* with the work of Greek philosophers.

Interest in Sanskrit

Sanskrit inspired growing interest in India. Europeans were thrilled by the "mysteries of Sanskrit". About 1780, Brahmins of Bengal were asked to translate into English their Sacred Scriptures. William Jones, a Calcutta High Court judge, bribed a Bengali Brahmin to translate the *Gita*. Jones discovered great affinity between Sanskrit and European languages.

The German youth was electrified by the Aryan race theory. Friedrich Schlegel learnt Sanskrit in Paris (1802-1803) and in a University of Cologne lecture said:

> "Everything, absolutely everything, is of Indian origin" (Leon Poliakov *Aryan Myth*, New American Library, 1977, p.191).

He praised the "wisdom of the Indians" and the "beauty and the antiquity of Sanskrit". He even went to the fantastic extent of declaring that the world's first and the greatest civilisation of Nile Valley (Egypt) was the work of Indians, meaning Brahmins.

Gorres further stretched this Aryan myth and called Aryans as "semitis of the Far East". He said Abraham came from Kashmir which he called as the birthplace of humanity and religion. Cruezer further extended this theory:

> "attributing Judaism to a primitive Brahminism which was a true natural religion. In his view Abraham-Brahma and Sara-Saraswati were Brahmins". (Poliakov Ibid p.193).

Schlegel echoing Jones said that all great nations "sprang from one stock... directly or indirectly of Indian origin". Traces of this genealogy could still be found in Germany or more precisely, in the German language. For instance "Arya" (Sanskrit: "noble") was surely cognate with "Ehre" (German: "honour") (Leon Poliakov Ibid. p.190).

Another scholar Schelling dismissed the worth of the West. "What is Europe really but a sterile trunk which owes everything to Oriental grafts?" (quoted by Leon Poliakov, Ibid p.195).

Max Muller travelled to London and discovered that the Oxford University Press had a full set of the Sanskrit characters necessary for printing the Vedas. By May 1848, he had settled in Oxford. The first volume of the Vedas appeared in 1849.

Misconception on Vedas

Martin Maw says only one failure marred his progress. In 1860, Monier Monier-Williams out-manoeuvered him in the election for the Boden Professorship of Sanskrit, setting in motion a great personal feud; but Muller had some compensation — not to say revenge - when a Chair of Comparative Philology was created at the University in 1868 in his honour. Barring one term's teaching at Strassburg University in 1872, he continued to work at Oxford for the rest of his life, equally at ease with Oriental scholars, visitors from India, William Ewart Gladstone, and members of the British royal family. A naturalised British citizen, he died in 1900.

Such was the personal and intellectual context in which Muller enunciated his Aryan hypothesis. He owed much in this to Schlegel, says Martin Maw (Ibid p.24). The Aryan race theory was purchased by many European scholars. Because, according to Muller:

> "Everybody interested in the origin and first development of language, thought, religion and social institutions, looked forward to the Veda as a new revelation". (Muller -4 p.187).

War on indigenous Indians

Perhaps, poor Max Muller did not realise that the entire Vedas are nothing but Aryan invocations to their gods to punish and destroy the original inhabitants of India. Aryans hated the native children of the soil because they were dark-skinned Dravidas and that they led a simple life. They were producers of wealth. But the alien Aryan destroyers of wealth killed the cattle of the natives for their food as beef-eaters. The over 85% of the Indian population considered the Aryan scriptures particularly their Vedas as poison. But the great German scholar sitting in London without ever visiting India was totally misled and caused one of the greatest tragedies in world history, namely popularising the Aryan myth which is the other name for racism.

George Smith, a noted historian of the missionary church, says Martin Maw, declared that "The English-speaking Aryans" had been providentially "trained to become the rulers of India and evangelizers of India", and cited the jurisprudent Henry Maine to the effect that the ordained task of "the youngest civilisation in the world was to instruct and correct the oldest". (George Smith: *The Conversion of India,* London 1893, pp.5/85).

British praise

Maw adds:

> A general history of the subcontinent, published in 1876, went even further, producing a fulsome description of Aryan attributes that likened the pre-Christian invasion of the sub-continent to the British influence in the present day. The Aryans had descended "from the highlands of Central Asia bringing with them the civilisation and the sword... The exquisite beauty of their Sanskrit muse as greatly transcended that of the aborigines as do the rich and melodious Greek-Latin tongues, the copious, but withal inharmonious, Teutonic.

If Sanskrit is so great a language why the Aryans themselves discarded it and took to English?

The Aryan religion was, in its poetic fancies, as far exalted above their crude systems of worship as the sublime teachings of Christianity soar above the doctrines of the code of Manu (Pearce, W.C.: *History of India,* 1876, p.119).

"Thus, Aryanism legitimised the British presence. Anglo-India had a familial right to rule the Orient and to rectify any shortcomings it perceived", says Martin Maw (Ibid. p.35).

Curse of India

The Aryan racist theory thus came as a curse to India and Indians. The Aryans might have welcomed the British to rule India because it suited them to further enslave the non-Aryan original inhabitants of India. Even today's Christians of India will not appreciate the Aryan zeal showed by their European missionaries, some of whom concentrated on the Aryans for conversion. The Aryan Brahmins who got converted to Christianity are today controlling the Indian church in which over 80% members are non-Aryans and hence victims of the Aryan-Christian race hatred inside the church. (Bishop Rev.Azariah: *Unchristian Side of the Indian Church*, Dalit Sahitya Akademy, 1989).

Sir William Hunter's Imperial Gazetteer of India (1881) referred to the Aryan as "the splendid... stock from which the Brahman, the Rajput, and the Englishman alike descend". (*Imperial Gazetteer*, 9 volumes, London 1881, IV p.192). A later edition of the *Gazetteer* (1907-1909) was even more circumspect.

Seeds of racism

Martin Maw says by this time Muller's credibility had been severely dented by rival Orientalists. Various components of his Aryan theory were seized and distorted by a lunatic fringe of "racial philosophers" and spiritualists (Ibid p.36). Refusing to court such opinion and aware that Muller was no longer an unimpeached authority, William Hunter modified his views:

> "Whether anything that can properly be described as an Aryan race ever existed .. or, whether the terms... is anything more than a philological expression... are questions which may for our present purpose be left unanswered". (Ibid, 26 Volumes, Oxford, 1907-1909-1, p.299).

That means the British themselves later started getting the heat of the Aryan racist theory and started realising that Max Muller and the Aryans have taken the British and other Europeans for a ride.

Brahminical terrorism against British

Martin Maw says:

> A notable example occurred in 1862, when Samuel Laing (1812-1897), Finance Member of the Govt. of India, attempted to reconcile British and Indian feeling in the wake of the Mutiny by giving a public lecture in Calcutta on the virtues of Aryan brotherhood. If he had not actually read Muller, Laing was certainly conversant with many of his theories: that language had onomatopoeic origins: that it reflected "the genius of a people": that the Aryan differed from the Semite by having a capacity for abstract thought. Further, he accepted that the two races so long separated meet once more... the younger brother has become the stronger, and takes his place as the head and protector of the family... we are here... on a sacred mission, to stretch out the right hand of aid to our weaker brother, who once far out-stripped us, but has now fallen behind in the race. (Laing, S: *Lecture on the Indo-European Languages and Races*, Calcutta-1862).

The Aryans scented the danger of christianisation and protested. This was the beginning of the brahminical terrorism against the British which the brahminical writers later described as the "rise of Indian nationalism".

Indian "nationalism" originated in Bengal where the "nationalists" murdered the Europeans. (Michael Edwards: *The Myth of the Mahatma*, Constable, London, 1986, p.199).

Those interested in a deeper study of Hindu nazism, described by the Brahminical Social Order as "Indian nationalism", may read a French scholar's masterly work on the subject: *The Hindu Nationalist Movement & Indian Politics - 1926 to the 1990.* (Christophe Jaffrelot, Penguin Books, India, 1999 pp. 580).

IV - Jews & the "Jews of India"

In the foregoing pages we have sufficiently argued how Brahminism is indeed the father of racism, fascism and nazism. Enough references from noted authorities on the subject have been also quoted and historical evidences cited.

Not only Brahminism is the father of the three - racism, fascism and nazism — but we have also said it is the father of zionism. A close similarity is found between Brahminism and the religion of Jews.

In the book, *Sociology of Revivalism (A Study of Indianisation, Sanskritisation and Golwalkarism)*, 1970, by Dr. K.K. Gangadharan, a noted social scientist who was the Head of the Department of Sociology of Christ College, Kanpur, (pages 166) Kalmakar Prakashan, 19/A, Theatre Communication Bldg., Connaught Circus, New Delhi -1, says (p.59):

> "Even a Brahmin caste like the Chitpavans of Maharashtra who have produced great orientalists and Brahminical scholars like Kane, Hindu protagonists like Tilak and Savarkar, great men like Ranade, Gokhale, Karve and Vinoba Bhave were said to be originally Jews who separated from fellow Jews settled in Colaba district of Maharashtra".
>
> (Linda Cox, *the Illustrated Weekly*, 15.3.1970 p.6). "Historians and anthropologists also confirm their foreign origin", he adds:

Bible of Hindu nazi party

Gangadharan finds good lot of similarity between Hitlerism and Golwalkarism, meaning the Hindu nazi philosophy developed by Golwalkar who was the second Chitpavan Brahmin to head of the Hindu nazi party called Rashtriya Swayamsevak Sangh (RSS). Golwalkar's book, *Bunch of Thoughts*, is considered the Bible of the Hindu nazi party which at the time of writing this is virtually ruling the country headed by its Hindu Nazi Prime Minister A.B. Vajpayee.

Gangadharan gives a comparative account of the salient features of the two systems — nazism of Hitler and Hindu nazism of Golwalkar (p. 100 to 103).

HITLERISM	GOLWALKARISM
*1. **Weltanschauung:*** Aggressive and totalitarian which according to *Mein Kampf* "is intolerant and cannot permit another to exist side by side with it. It imperiously demands its own recognition as unique and exclusive and a complete transformation in accordance with its views throughout all the branches of public life" (Adolf Hitler, *Mein Kampf*, p.378).	***Weltanschauung:*** Aggressive totalitarian. Believes that ancient Hindu way of life - its customs, rites, beliefs and heroes as interpreted by Golwalkar - is the only legitimate way of life in India. No other pattern tolerated; those who differ from it are traitors.
*2. **Parliamentary democracy:*** Political parties in parliamentary democracy make compromises and are opportunists.	***Parliamentary democracy:*** Political parties in parliamentary democracy make compromises and are opportunists.
3. Volk Staat: Only the Aryans are real folk or community governed by aristocratic principles within the community. The ordinary concept of State based on economic and political needs of people, including all the people of the State, territory is absurd. Race is the foundation of the State.	***Hindu Nation:*** Hindu (Aryans) governed by the principles of caste system are the nation and none else. Territorial nationalism which looks upon all the people — refugees like Parsis and invaders like Muslims and Christians as part of the nation — is absurd. Hindu is the positive content of nationhood.
*4. **Germanization:*** True Germanization is possible only "if that process could change the blood of the people". Since this is impossible and mixture of	***Indianization or Hinduization:*** is possible because it is a matter of changing of life's outlook, customs, gods and celebrations. The race and blood is the same

blood would lead to debasement of superior race, it is opposed.

and hence it must be done.

5. ***Aggressiveness and Scapegoatism:*** Jews have undermined the German civilization. Ideas like "democracy", "majority", "conscience of the world", "world solidarity", "world peace" etc. disintegrate our race consciousness and breed cowardice. (Adolf Hitler, *My New Order*, p.45).

Aggressiveness and Scapegoatism: Muslims, Christians and Communists etc., are undermining the country. Ideas like "internationalism", "equality", "world unity", "coexistence", "neutrality", "Hindu-Muslim unity", "peace", "non-violence", are damaging the Hindu nation and making a nation of imbeciles and cowards.

6. ***Vengeance:*** Jew has to be made powerless. Germans cannot be friends of traitors. We demand vengeance.

Vengeance: Minorities, especially the Muslims, are not to be pampered lest they might harm the nation a second time. They should be told that Moghul Badshahi is over. We cannot forget or forgive the insult to the motherland. "We are here to unsettle the partition".

7. ***Population Control:*** Opposition to "practical prevention of procreation among millions of our best people", while it is possible for the most depraved degenerates to propagate themselves.

Population control: Opposition to population control among the Hindus while the Muslims are procreating themselves indiscriminately and thus endangering the Hindu nation. (The theme of a speech delivered to RSS audience by a provincial boss).

8. ***Racial Ethics:*** An ethical ideal has no right to prevail "if it endangers the existence of a race that is the standard bearer of a higher ethical ideal. For in a world which would be composed of

Racial Ethics: Ethical ideas like personal character and *Dharma* should be made subordinate to the cause of Hindu society. If it were in the service of Hindus anything can be done irrespective of moral standards like truthful-

mongrels and negroids all ideals of human beauty and nobility and all hopes for an idealized future of our humanity would be lost forever". (Adolf Hitler, *Mein Kempf*, p.321).

ness and loyalty. The *Rakshasas*, *Mlechhas* and traitors should be destroyed by any means to establish righteousness all over the world.

This comparison between the two philosophies makes it clear that Hindu nazism is nothing but Hitler's nazism. This is the secret of the White Western racists' love and admiration for India's Aryan brahminical racists.

Gangadharan then goes to give the Chitpavan background (p.105):

> The Chitpavan Brahmins were a small group of farmers and priests settled in the Ratnagiri district. "A history of the Bene Israelis, who settled in the Colaba district of Konkan, claim Chitpavans as fellow Jews who became separated from the shipmates", he says quoting from Linda Cox. (*The Illustrated Weekly of India*, 22.2.1970, 'Chitpavans').

Jews become Brahmins

Gangadharan continues:

Traditionally, Chitpavans explain their origin on the basis of the story in *Sahyadri Khanda* which goes like this

> "... at that time the bodies of fourteen shipwrecked foreigners were cast upon the shore of the sea, Parasurama purified those corpses by burning them on a funeral pyre, or *chita*, restored them to life, and taught them Brahmin rites".

(L.P. Maureen Patterson, *Structure and Change in Indian Society*, Editors: Singer and Kohn, p.399).

That is how the Jews became Chitpavans, says Gangadharan and adds:

> The brahminical tradition in a way corroborates their probable Jewish origin. Predominance of blue eyes, fair complexion and other physical features have made the anthropologists and historians think of their foreign origin. The Konkan was known

for its trade contact with almost all countries of the West. "It is this stretch of coast, too, which received at one time or another such emigrant groups as the Bene Israel, Parsis, Kudaldeskar Brahmins, Gaud Saraswat Brahmins and Chitpavan Brahmins... each of these groups has been an intrusive group, physically and culturally, and differentiated from the others as well as from the population into which they came... The Chitpavans were apparently the last to arrive". (Ibid p.399).

However, they were an unknown and obscure group until about 1708 AD when one of them gradually got the favours of the Maratha King Shahu (grandson of Shivaji) and finally rose to the position of a Peshwa or Prime Minister. The appointment of Balaji Vishwanath Bhat as Peshwa was a turning point in the history of Chitpavans; their fortune changed from obscurity to limelight.

Hindus hail Hitler

Gangadharan finds good lot of similarities between the Chitpavan Brahmins and the Jews. And this may be the secret of the Chitpavan admiration for Jews though M.S. Golwalkar, also a Chitpavan Brahmin, had also admired Hitler and in his book, *We or Our Nationhood Defined* (1938), had hailed Hitler's massacre of Jews.

That the very admirers of Hitler, who is alleged to have put millions of Jews to gas chamber in Germany, have now joined hands with the Jews is another story but the "Jews of India" are not bothered about this contradiction in their behaviour nor are the Jews interested in reminding the "Jews of India" about the "Aryan Myth" that caused their mass annihilation. The two have today become strange bed fellows. This is yet another unique character of the two peoples.

How Jews forgot their killers

The religions of the two are also unique in the sense that they are not at all universalistic. Anybody can become a Muslim, Christian, Sikh, Budhist. But not a Brahmin or a Jew. You have to be born into it. There is nothing like a converted Brahmin or a converted Jew. A Brahmin or Jew is one who is a born

Brahmin or a born Jew. In that way, they have no parallel in the world. Hence they are a unique people.

We are not able to understand how the Jews, who have produced such great thinkers and philosophers like Karl Marx, Einstein, Leon Poliakov etc., are not able to understand that they are being taken for a ride by India's Aryan brahminical forces whose philosophy of Brahminism had supplied the philosophical inspiration to produce Hitler and nazism that allegedly caused the death and destruction of millions of Jews in Germany and caused two World Wars. And that too within such a short time of 50 years or so. We are sure there must be many Jews alive today who have personally experienced Hitler's nazi Holocaust in Germany. Such Jews may be either in Israel or outside. So, we can't say that the great Jewish people have forgotten the past. Leon Poliakov's book was written after the Second World War ended and he had written us only a couple of years back reminding us of the *Aryan Myth* behind Hitler's nazism.

That is how we are indeed shocked by the silence of Leon Poliakov, considered France's most famous historian, who had once taken objection to our calling India's Aryan Brahmins as the "Jews of India."

Hatred of Muslims

We are happy that we have finally proved correct because the Jews of the world and Israel in particular have joined hands with the "Jews of India". Only yesterday, hardly 50 years ago, India's Aryan brahminical people had supplied their symbol of *swastika* to Hitler and had hailed Hitler as an *avatar*, and also had congratulated him for this mass murder of Jews and promised a red-carpet welcome to India hoping that Hitler would win the Second World War. But within 50 years, yesterday's enemies have become the best of friends to jointly oppress Dalits, India's Black Untouchables, the original inhabitants of India, and Muslims of the world. India has the world's largest (after Indonesia) and yet the worst persecuted Muslim population.

We can understand that the common masses of Jews may not know that it is India's Aryan brahminical forces that inspired Hitler and his nazis to annihilate the Jews. But we can't believe that the Jewish leadership of Israel has forgotten this. Even when we reminded the Israeli Ambassador in Delhi through a letter about all this he was silent on this vital aspect in his reply. (*Dalit Voice* Nov.16, 1993 p.11: "Letters to Editor" column).

Leon Poliakov's extraordinary book, *Aryan Myth*, was published by a Foundation set up by the Jews to make a research into the forces behind the nazi massacre of Jews. His research revealed that Hitler's nazism was inspired solely by Brahminism. Since India's Dalits are also victims of Brahminism, we had then thanked Poliakov for digging deep into the roots of Brahminism and he remained as a subscriber of our journal, *Dalit Voice*, for some years and also an admirer of our work in India.

Greatness of Jews

Jews are not duds like the Indian rulers. They have solid achievements to their credit. Many Nobel Laureates, world famous scholars. The Israeli intelligence network, Mossad, is one of the best in the world. Major newspapers, news agencies, radio, TV network are owned and run by them. (*Dalit Voice* Nov.1, 2001 p.5: "*Do you know in world's most open society zionists control entire media?*") How to believe that the Jews are not aware of the brahminical mischief?

The only conclusion we can derive is that yesterday's enemies have joined hands today to fight their common enemy -the Muslims. Israel has occupied the land of Palestine Muslims and hence Jews are considered usurpers.

India's brahminical rulers, who are also usurpers and aliens in India, are engaged in a life and death battle against the original inhabitants – Dalits, the Black Untouchables of India. And in our defence against this Aryan aggression, we are being supported by Muslims whose religion of Islam stands for egalitarianism and universal brotherhood. Islam directs its followers to support the struggle of the oppressed (*Mustadafeen*) who are none but Dalits. Islam is totally opposed to racism, nazism, fascism, whereas Brahminism is sanctified racism and graded inequality. Its anti-woman, anti-human character has converted India into the world's most violent country.

So, to fight the Dalits and Muslims, India's brahminical rulers have joined hands with Jews who too are facing a similar enemy of Blacks and Muslims in the West.

US as world policeman

It is this deep-rooted hatred arising out of racism that united the Aryan brahminical forces with the Jews and other White Western racists on a common platform to re-establish the brahminical *Varnashrama Dharma* (racism) with graded inequality over the whole world. The White Western racists and their zionist masters are convinced that only the brahminical poisonous weapon can combat the Blacks and Muslims. This is the secret of the Indian ruler's support to the New World Order which is aimed at hoisting the US as the world policeman guided by Brahminism.

History does not reveal any major clashes between Jews and Muslims. All through, the Jews had clashes only with Christians. If they had any clash with Muslims, it was a minor one. Hitler and the nazis who massacred the Jews were Christians. Muslims did not do that. The two World Wars were fought between the Christians. Muslims were not in the picture.

But the moment the Second World War ended with the defeat of Hitler, Jews and Christians not only became friends but jointly persecuted the Muslims and committed aggression on Palestine.

Christian world enslaved

India's Aryan brahminical forces took advantage of this dramatic turn of events and jumped into this anti-Muslim bandwagon — hiding all their past misdeeds against Jews. The zionist forces, having finished the Christians and enslaved them, are now out to finish the Muslims. The Sept.11, 2001 "terrorist attack" on the US, allegedly a conspiracy of the zionists, was aimed at forcing the enslaved Christian world led by America to fight Muslim and Islam. America, being fully controlled by zionist forces, has become a willing slave of the zionists. Under zionist dictates, the US bombarded and destroyed Afghanistan. Its next targets are Iraq and Iran. In Palestine, the US has given up all its neutrality and is openly siding with zionists in their reckless destruction and death of Palestinians. As of today the entire White Western Christian world has plunged into a blind life and death battle against Muslims and Islam while the latter lacks the military capacity to harm the interests of the mighty Christian or Jewish forces.

No Muslim country is a nuclear power except Pakistan. No Muslim country is an industrial giant comparable to any White Western Christian world power. Even the United Nations is purchased to side with the West led by America. The only wealth some Muslim countries possess, oil, is managed by the Western experts only. Muslim countries lack that unity to think of any attack on the West. The latest Gulf War has proved this. In the 2001 US war against Afghanistan, almost every Muslim country pledged support to the war. Pakistan became the base for US attacks on Afghanistan.

Break-up of Soviet Union

When that is the case, we are not able to understand the phobia that has gripped the White Western racist Christians and zionists who today are playing havoc in the entire Muslim world. Iraq somehow withstood the Gulf War which was nothing but a cold-blooded aggression committed by the US supported by other White Western Christian countries and zionists.

Even the break-up of Soviet Russia was to annex the White Russians to the Western camp and isolate the other Muslim republics of USSR. Russian racism played a major part in destroying the Soviet Union which used to be a trusted ally of the African and Muslim countries to face the Western bully.

Recent actions of these White Christians and zionists make us suspect that they have fallen a victim to the Aryan brahminical Hindu nazism which is built on a horrible hate philosophy - hatred against India's Black Untouchables and Muslims.

Islam as religion of Blacks

White Western Christians and also zionists hate the Blacks and Muslims. In Africa, US and other countries many Blacks have become Muslims. Africa is virtually a Muslim continent. Some Blacks even go to the extent of saying that Islam is the religion of the Blacks.

Dalits are India's Black Untouchables. Africans and Dalits have a common origin. Dalits constitute 20% of the Indian population. Together with the Tribals (10%), who are our own people but artificially divided from us, we make up 30% of the population.

To this must be added a much bigger chunk of population (35%) described in the Constitution of India as Backward Castes (BCs). They are also Dravidians, original inhabitants of India. The three segments — Dalits, Tribals and BCs — make up a staggering 65% of India's 1,000 million population.

Serpent & mongoose

India's Muslims, who constitute 15% of the population, did not come from Arabia or Turkey, Iran. They are all converts from the above three segments and hence our own blood brothers.

Unable to bear the brahminical persecution they sought salvation through Islam. They may be one of the worst persecuted lot in India but they are offering a stiff fight to the Aryans because the religion of Brahminism and Islam are like mongoose and serpent.

Then come Christians (2.5%) and Sikhs (2%) who too are our own flesh of the flesh and bone of the bone — with minor exceptions.

That means we, the non-Aryans, make up over 85% of the population which is today reeling under the brahminical war and violence ever since "independence" (1947) that helped the Aryans to clamp their Hindu nazi imperialism over India.

To sum up, the White Western Christians guided by the zionists have launched a bloody war and violence on Blacks, Muslims and Yellows inspired by the brahminical philosophy which for the past over 3,000 years is doing the same job in India

Hence did we not prove right, dear Leon Poliakov, when we described the Aryan brahminical forces as the "Jews of India"? Did we not prove right when we said that Brahminism is the father of racism, fascism, nazism and even zionism?

V - Brahminism as Enemy No.1 of the Whole World

Dr. Babasaheb Ambedkar, the greatest Indian after the Budha, had identified Brahminism as the principal contradiction facing India. And this has been elaborated, explained and the different steps, ways and means to eliminate this principal contradiction facing the country, outlined in the different writings and speeches of thinkers and scholars right from the days of the Budha. Every social and cultural movement that India had since the Aryan invasion was essentially anti-brahminical. Every leader who worked for social transformation had identified the Brahminical Social Order (BSO) as the principal enemy facing the country.

Threatening international peace

That Brahminism is endangering India is well known. But what is not sufficiently known is that Brahminism has started threatening international peace as well. The international ramifications of Brahminism, more and more evident these days, are explained in this chapter.

The above statement naturally invited lot of inquiries not only from India but even outside.

> "How do you say that Brahminism is the Enemy No.1 of the whole world? What are the historical proofs to say that Hitler's nazism was inspired by the Indian Aryans? How did Brahminism assume so much of importance to attract the attention of the world's greatest scholars and philosophers? What is the greatness of Brahminism that attracted the Europeans? How do you say that Brahminism will cause another world war? On what basis you say that both the White Western racism and zionism derived their inspiration from Brahminism?"

Such questions have come in plenty from baffled readers.

In the absence of any one single word to refer to the Aryan

Sanskrit Sacred Books which created the religion of *Sanatana Dharma* /Arya Dharma, we are using the word "Brahminism" which represents the quintessence of the thoughts found in the *Vedas, Gita, Manusmriti, Arthasastra,* the Epics etc.

Fake doctors

We begin from India. Different doctors - gandhism, marxism, Jayaprakash Narayan's *sarvodaya,* naxalism and all sorts of isms — came and they could not diagnose the disease afflicting the Indians. All of them proved a failure and the affected people were disappointed. Their diseases became more serious.

Why all these doctors failed? Because they had no academic qualification. They were fakes.

Swami Vivekananda, Dayananda Saraswati, M.K. Gandhi, Jawahar Lal Nehru, Sardar Patel, E.M.S. Namboodiripad, S.A. Dange, Jayaprakash Narayan, Vinoba Bhave were all Aryans/ upper castes and knew nothing of India's pre-Aryan original inhabitants whom they considered as their enemies.

The non-Aryans, meaning the non-Hindu original inhabitants, form over 85% of India's population.

Muslims 15%	Scheduled Castes 20%
Christians 2.5%	Scheduled Tribes .. 10%
Sikhs 2.5%	Backward Castes . 35%
20 +	65% Total: 85%.

Hindus, therefore, are less than 15% of the Indian total population.

These doctors who came pretending to save India's vast (non-Hindu) indigenous peoples were not only not qualified but more than that they had no heart to examine and probe the peculiar but simple ailment of the (non-Hindu) SC/ST/BCs (Scheduled Castes, Scheduled Tribes and Backward Castes) and religious "minorities" (Muslims, Christians, Sikhs, Budhists etc.).

Indian problem is not poverty

Why do we call them fake and heartless doctors?

1. Being Aryans/Hindus (hence aliens) they had no knowledge of the simple lives of the natives.
2. And being Aryans they deliberately included the non-Hindus with Hindus and just to complicate and aggravate their simple disease, which was not at all serious, they wrongly diagnosed it causing all sorts of complications.
3. Having made a wrong diagnosis, they gave a wrong medicine further worsening the disease. Because of this billions of innocent, helpless SC/ST/BCs and minorities died though they suffered from no serious disease.

That is why we call these "doctors" fake as well as heartless.

These Gandhis, Nehrus, Danges, Namboodiripads just to complicate our simple disease deliberately diagnosed the disease as "poverty" and gave us all sorts of deadly drugs. And because of this heavy drugging many SC/ST/BCs were incapacitated and many died.

What did these Aryan/Hindu/*savarna* doctors do?

1. They came to our people — simple innocent SC/ST/BCs - without being called by our people. Uninvited.
2. Having come, they attributed all sorts of diseases, exaggerated the ailment. And having given wrong and deadly drugs, they are responsible for murdering millions of our innocent people.

The only genuine Mahatma

But it was Mahatma Jyotirao Phule, a Backward Caste leader from Maharashtra, who was the first in the 19th century to correctly diagnose our disease. Not only he diagnosed the disease but he supplied the right drugs which were not only simple but cheap and inexpensive.

And what was his diagnosis?

His diagnosis was that the SC/ST/BCs were attacked by a pestilence called Brahminism.

And that is why Jyotirao Phule (1827-1890) is hailed as India's one and the only genuine Mahatma.

Renaming Marathwada University

Why he is the only genuine Mahatma? Because he was the first to so loudly, so accurately and so prominently diagnose our disease. And that is why the people themselves conferred upon him the title of Mahatma. The people don't consider anybody else as Mahatma.

Please note that when we talk of Brahminism., we don't refer to Brahmins though a good part of them do subscribe to this philosophy. There is no Brahminism without the Brahmin.

For example, Sharad Pawar, today's topmost Maratha leader who is also an upholder of Brahminism, is not a Brahmin. It was Sharad Pawar when he was the Chief Minister, the Maharashtra legislature passed a resolution to rename the Marathwada University after Dr. Babasaheb Ambedkar. But after passing the resolution, he went back on the promise. He cheated the people because he is a supporter of Brahminism though he is not a Brahmin. And despite being a Maratha whose great hero, Chatrapati Shivaji, was the victim of Brahminism, Sharad Pawar did not stop serving Brahminism.

Again, Bal Thackeray is not a Brahmin but belongs to the slave caste of *shudras*. He is a Kayasth, born out of the *papayoni*. Despite this, he is heading a Hindu nazi party (Shiv Sena). And despite being punished seriously by the Brahmins, he continues to eat their shit.

Anti-Muslim hysteria

Brahminism, therefore, is not confined to Brahmins alone. So, the Brahmins need not think that they alone are being singled out. Our quarrel is only with Brahminism and not Brahmins. We hate no individual. We hate only the system — Brahminism — because we are its victims.

Some people think that Brahminism is confined only to India. No. Brahminism has become an international problem. (*Dalit Voice* June 15, 1992 p.17, Christa Schwab: "*Brahminic poison conquers whole world*").

How can we say that Brahminism is an international problem? Are we trying to exaggerate? No. We mean what we say and we are in the company of world famous authorities who have said the very same thing.

Truth is so much suppressed in India and the world over that when it is spoken, it appears as falsehood. That is because falsehood appears as truth. All of us are fed on so much of falsehood that it is difficult for us to accept truth. The West controls the entire global media that it seldom allows the truth to come out. The Gulf War has proved it.

The anti-Muslim hysteria raised by America following the Sept.11, 2001 "terrorist" attack on it and the devastating war it launched on the poor, starving Afghanistan has further proved the total media control in the hands of White Western racist rulers and their zionist masters.

Four ruling concepts

Four concepts are today ruling the whole world and they are:

1. Man is superior to woman.
2. White is superior to Black.
3. Merit comes out of birth.
4. Might is right.

The whole world is made to believe in these four concepts — communist or non-communist. White, Black, Brown or Yellow. First, Second or Third World. These four concepts rule the world.

And on the basis of these concepts the "Clash of Civilisations" theory was evolved by Prof. Samuel P. Huntington (*The Clash of Civilizations & the Remaking of World Order*, Samuel P. Huntington, Penguin Books-1997) and two Gulf Wars were launched in 1990. And later in 2001, it was further enlarged denouncing the entire Muslims as terrorists and a war was declared against Islam. (*Dalit Voice* Editorial Dec.16, 2001: "*It is now all-out war on Muslims: Clash of Cross & Crescent leads to III World War?*).

George W. Bush, who took over as the President of US from Clinton, further enlarged this "Clash of Civilisations" by denouncing the Muslims as "terrorists" and giving all-out support to Israel to destroy Palestine.

These four dangerous concepts have brought about two World Wars and a Third World War is getting ready. How did it happen?

German quarrel with Pope

The Germans, who always wanted to be different from the other Europeans, had a quarrel with the Pope and challenged his authority over the entire Christian world. The Germans were searching for a philosophical basis for challenging the authority of the Pope, his authority over the entire Christian world and his hegemony. Martin Luther, who called Pope anti-Christ, gave it a religious touch and hordes of philosophers — Nietzsche, Max Weber, Herder, Goethe and many more - gave it a philosophical touch. The Protestant Christian church took birth in Germany.

F.L. Carsten in his book, *The Rise of Fascism* (Mathuen & Co., London-1967), says that German racism:

> "often went hand in hand with a veneration of blood and soil, with an Aryan mysticism, neo-paganism and rejection of Christianity ...." (p.31). Hitler was horrified by reading the *Protocols of the Elders of Zion*, said to be the secret Jewish book of conspiracy which uncovers the essence and activity of the Jewish people with an almost horrid certainty and

> exposes them in their inner connections as well as their ultimate aims. (p. 118).

Hitler as an *avatar*

All these German philosophers in search of a philosophical base for their thoughts found a solution in the brahminical literature of India. The Western philosophers of fascism borrowed heavily from the brahminical Sanskrit literature. Finally the German philosophers of fascism gave birth to Adolf Hitler who openly acknowledged that his nazism was based on Brahminism. Hitler called himself an Aryan. (Nicholas Goodrick-Clarke: *Hitler's Priestess, Savitri Devi, The Hindu Aryan Myth & Neo-Nazism,* reviewed in the *Time of India,* March 19, 1999).

The leader of the fascist "German Christian" movement, Ludwig Moller, said:

> "Adolf Hitler has been sent by god to save the fatherland".

Hitler was praised by India's Brahmins who declared that god had sent Hitler to re-establish their *Sanatana Dharma.* Hitler himself believed in his divine mission. Hans Heinz Ewers, a German scholar, became the chief official ideological exponent of the Aryan nazi movement of Hitler.

Swastika borrowed from Brahmins

Hitler's emblem, *swastika,* so common in every Hindu home in India, was borrowed from the Brahmin scriptures. Sanskrit was taught in German schools. And Brahmins learnt German and started preparing a red-carpet welcome to Hitler.

Every hate philosophy must have an enemy. Just as a weak people and a weak philosophy must have an enemy to divert the attention and deceive the people, like India's Brahminical Social Order having made Muslims their enemies, Hitler declared Jews as his enemies.

And because of this nazi hate philosophy millions of Jews were put to gas chamber and killed in Hitler's Germany (Leon Poliakov, *The Aryan Myth,* New American Library, 1301-Avenue

Americas, New York, NY-10019, USA pp.338, 1977). In his book, the author has traced the roots of racism and proved that India's Brahmins and their Brahminism fooled even the Germans and thus became the founders of fascism. The *Aryan Myth* of Leon Poliakov, a Russian born Jewish writer and a top historian of France, was published by Columbus Centre, a British Foundation that was founded to investigate the inspiration behind the German nazi killing of Jews. Hence the *Aryan Myth* can be taken as the official opinion of the Jewish think tank.

The findings of Leon Poliakov are that Brahminism can be safely called the mother of nazism and mother of racism.

The Japanese joined hands with Hitler because the then Japanese ruling class was also fascist, imperialist and racist. Even today, after becoming the world's no.2 economic power, the Japanese ruling class has not stopped its nazi discrimination against Burakumin and its own women. Despite the Hiroshima bombings and killing of thousands of Japanese in the II World War, the Japanese ruling class joined hands with America and joined the US-led "anti-terrorist" (read anti-Muslim) war in 2001.

Vocabulary of nazis

What is the vocabulary, catch words, of these nazis and racists:

> Superman, purity of blood, White-principle, chosen people, merit and efficiency, master race and slave race, survival of the fittest, might is right, intelligence is hereditary, market economy, free competition, globalisation, theory of natural selection. Aryans are masters of the universe, purity and pollution, pedigree, ruling class, divine ancestry, family background, culture goes with blood, Whiteman's burden, White race holds the monopoly of beauty, intelligence and strength, inequalities of the intellectual capacities of the races, king can do no wrong, Black is ugly and crooked.

We have repudiated every one of these theories in our book, *Merit, My Foot* (Dalit Sahitya Akademy -1996).

The following proverbs ridiculing women are there in almost every country:

> A woman's brain cannot perceive anything further than the handle of a spoon — **Sri Lanka**.
>
> There are only two places for a woman, the house and the grave — **Pakistan**.
>
> An unmarried girl must obey her father, a married woman her husband, and a widow her children — **Japan**.
>
> He who listens to the advice of a woman is a fool — **Sri Lanka**.
> The best way to keep a woman is barefoot in the winter and pregnant in the summer — **America**.
>
> A woman's place is in the home — **America**.
>
> The thoughts of a woman are afterthoughts — **Sri Lanka**.
>
> No matter how skilled a woman may be in mathematics, her judgement will always be second-rate — **Sri Lanka**.
>
> Bringing up a daughter is like manuring and watering a plant for someone else's courtyard _**Telugu Proverb**.
>
> Do not tell your wife anything that cannot be said in public — **Ghanian proverb.**

All those who believe in racism, fascism, nazism, Brahminism hold the above opinions on women. The origin of all this is Brahminism and the Brahmin Sacred Scriptures are full of such references.

Hating woman in Japan

Racism is also responsible for the claim of man that he is intellectually superior to woman. The nazi contempt for woman was demonstrated in holding the institution of marriage as false and German women asked to produce children for the "Fatherland" outside the wedlock. This again is an Aryan contribution and the *Manu Smriti* which made even the Brahmin women suffer at the hands of their menfolk and reduced woman to a second-grade position in India. A Japanese woman, Shigego Tanabe, worried about the discrimination against women by Japanese men, traced the cause to *Manu Smriti* (*Dalit Voice* Oct.16, 1983).

We had cited the authority of an eminent Japanese scholar, Kazuteru Okiura, saying the concept of pollution, which is responsible for the discrimination against Barukumin in Japan, was the gift of Hinduism. Bagwan Das, an Indian advocate of Delhi, in his testimony before the Human Rights Commission (*Dalit Voice* Oct.16 and Nov.1, 1983) had referred to the international ramifications of Hinduism, the modern name of Brahminism.

Western praise for Ramayana

All these theories on women are found in the brahminical literature: The *Vedas*, the *Manu Smriti*, *Arthasastra*, *Gita* etc. All those philosophers of fascism in Europe have acknowledged that they based their theories solely on India's brahminical literature. Therefore, we will be perfectly right if we call Brahminism as the founding father of world racism and the hate philosophy of nazism. That is why we use the word "nazi" to identify all those people afflicted by brahminical thoughts.

Gobineau spoke about the racial superiority of the Aryans. H.S. Chamberlain about the superiority of the Teutons. Michelet, speaking about the *Ramayana*, wrote in 1864:

> "Whoever has done or will too much, let him drink from this deep cup a long drought of life and youth."

Since the time of Voltaire, that is since shortly before the French Revolution, writers and scholars, philosophers and poets, voiced similar opinions that Europe has become too "narrow" for them, that a rejuvenation can only come from the East, says Alex Aronson in his book, *Europe Looks at India* (Hind Kitabs, Bombay-1946).

Varna means skin colour

A Prussian junker of the old regime, Kayserling, was a great admirer of Brahminism. He glorified the Hindu mysticism and mythology (Count Von Kayserling: *Travels Journal of a Philosopher*).

The *Vedanta* advocates capitalism and market economy. And that is how our Hindu *gurus* have become so famous and fabulously rich catering to their Western disciples teaching open sex, drugs, violence, consumerism and quick money to enjoy the life. That is how India's ruling upper castes are in deep love with the West and vice-versa. That is how the brahminical fascist philosophy fascinated the White Western racists advocating the cult of the superiority of the White races and praised India's *varna* vultures.

The religion of Hinduism (Brahminism) was earlier known as *Varnashrama Dharma* or *Chatur Varna* meaning a religion based on skin colour. Says G.S. Ghurye, a noted social scientist and an authority on India's caste and race:

> "The *Shatapatha Brahmana*.... describes the four classes as four *varnas*. *Varna* means colour and it was in this sense that the world seems to have been employed in contrasting the *Arya* and *Dasa*, referring to their fair and dark colours respectively. The colour-connotation of the word was, so strong that later on when the classes came to be regularly described as *varnas*, four different colours were assigned to four different classes by which their members were supposed to be distinguished". (G.S. Ghurye: *Caste & Race in India*, 1999, Popular Prakashana, 1999 p. 46).

Racism originated in India

Long, long before racism gripped the White Western people, racism was widespread in India which is the motherland of racism. The Aryan brahminical people, the founding fathers of racism, exported racism from India. Racism is so deep-rooted in the Indian soil that its dark-skinned Dravidas and Adi-Dravidas (the Black Untouchables of India) are its worst victims.

Finally in the year 2001, the Black Untouchables of India took their case to the United Nations and the UN World Conference Against Racism held at Durban debated the issue. For the first time the world was shocked to know (in the year 2001) that racism originated in India and that Brahminism is the founding father of racism. (*Dalit Voice*, Editorial of Oct.1, 2001: "*World comes to know of racism in Hindu India: Gang of Three stand isolated at Durban conference*").

German love for India

The British people were the first to begin a systematic study of Sanskrit and Indian civilisation because they had very definite material interests in the East. The first Sanskrit scholars and Indologists were either British Government officials or missionaries.

Indology received amazing impetus in Germany during the Napoleonic wars. It was a rejuvenated middle class that looked towards the East for a new inspiration, says Alex Aronson (*Europe Looks at India*, Hind Kitabs, Bombay-1946).

Issac Taylor in his book, *The Origin of Aryans* (Bahri Publishers, 57-Sant Nagar, Delhi-65, 1980) says it was the German scholar, Max Muller, who did more than anybody else to popularise the race theory of Aryans.

Leon Poliakov also says that Max Muller is the distinguished godfather of the Aryan myth. Though he never visited India, he translated the entire Sanskrit literature into English (*Sacred Literature of the East*) sitting in London thereby influencing the British also. "Max Muller Bhavans" in India became the centres of brahminical activities. And Brahmins gave a sanskritised name for Max Muller as *Moksha Mullaru*.

Julian Huxley, the distinguished British scientist, in his book, *We Europeans* (Jonathan Cape, 1935), speaks about the havoc played by the Aryans and their race theory.

Voltair had the greatest praise for the brahminical literature (Aronson Ibid. p.17). Not many years after the publication of Voltaire's books another Frenchman set foot on the shores of India, Abbe Dubois. After a stay of 31 years in South India, he became a great admirer of Hindu religion and its caste system which he described as one of the greatest achievements of ancient Indian civilisation. (Abbe Dubois: *Hindu Manners, Customs and Ceremonies,* AES, C-2/15, SDA, New Delhi-16, 1983-reprint),

Another admirer of brahminical philosophy was Sir William Jones, the founder of the Asiatic Society of Bengal, who translated the *Shakuntala* (1789), the *Gita Govinda,* and Manu's law books into English. Three years later in 1791, Friedrich Schlegel wrote the *Language and Wisdom of the Indians* (1808) which constitutes the first German contribution to Indology. He learnt Sanskrit from an English officer, Alexander Hamilton, in 1803 while they were both interned together in Paris.

German obsession with Sanskrit

Germans were the most obsessed with Brahminism. From the 19th century Indology became largely a province of German scholarship. Many German writers found some kind of mysterious affinity between the German and the Indian mind (Aronson, Ibid. p. 47). Leopold von Schroeder was the other eminent scholar who fell in love with India and its pre-occupation with the supernatural caste system.

We really wonder how Europe's most brilliant people, the Germans, were literally taken for a ride by India's brahminical forces. Be that as it may, the Indian pests took full advantage of German interest, and that is why many honest Germans resent the use of our expression "Hindu nazis" to denote the brahminical forces.

Till the beginning of the 19th century the literatures of Greece and Rome had the sole powerful influence on the West including Germany. It was mainly after Napoleon that the new German middle classes became aware of the existence of their own language and civilisation. Soon, India became part of Germany's spiritual heritage. Indians, meaning the Brahmins, were hailed as a super-race of "pure" Aryans. (Aronson, Ibid p.49).

Hegel & Goethe criticise Brahmins

The brahminical religion attracted the Germans. Goethe's early enthusiasm for the *Shakuntala*, his feeble attempts to study the *Gita* and to master the *Devanagari* script are part of this phobia.

However in the later part of his life Goethe "turns back on India". (Aronson, Ibid p.60). He gradually starts hating the brahminical stuff passed on to him as Eastern philosophy. He was totally disillusioned with Brahminism and denounced the Brahmin institution of caste system as unjust.

After writing so much on India, Hegel in his final days saw through the brahminical game and started discovering the truth. He considered India "to be prototype of a civilisation condemned to death by its own inability to create something new out of the ruins of antiquity". (Aronson, Ibid p.83). He was worried about the lack of morality among Brahmins. Commenting on the Brahmins, he says:

> "They only eat and sleep... Whenever they take part in public life, they show themselves avaracious, deceiving, and voluptuous... An honest man among them is unknown to me...."
>
> "Indeed India is no nation at all, but a tyranny". (Aronson, Ibid p.86).

Sir William Jones, an Englishman, made his own contribution to Indology. The most eminent among the 19th century philosophers, Hegel, deserves a special mention. In his *Philosophy of World History* (1822-23), published while Goethe was still alive, he devotes a whole chapter to India.

White is superior

Count Gobineau's book, *The Inequality of the Human Races* (1853), had a far reaching effect on all the subsequent racial theories which later flooded Europe. His "thesis" is that the White race is superior to all other races on earth and his conclusion as regards the "history" of India bears a very close resemblance to that of Hegel.

Gobineau has the first among the great 19th century scholars in Europe who praised the caste system (*Varnashrama Dharma*) and the "superiority of the ancient social organisation in India over the present one". Therefore, he can be rightly called the father of 19th century racism. According to his extraordinary evaluation Budhism is nothing but a degenerated kind of Hinduism. Only the "lowest castes" have taken to Budhism while "Brahminism represented in India the true supremacy of the White principle" (Aronson Ibid p.90).

Only the "pure" Aryans appreciate beauty. The Black and the Yellow could not comprehend anything else but ugliness; it is for them that ugliness was invented and will always remain necessary, he said. We can clearly see the sparks of racism.

The theory of "Clash of civilisations", referred to earlier, is an extension of this theory and that is how it declares a war on the Blacks (Africans and India's Black Untouchables), Yellows (China) and the Brown race of Muslims. A virtual war on the last three races has already begun.

Nietzsche praise for Brahmins

Schopenhauer became first acquainted with India in 1813 during a stay at Weimar. Goethe's friend, the Orientalist Friedrich Majer, introduced him to the "hidden treasurers" of brahminical thought. His enthusiasm for the *Upanishads* knew no bounds. His constant references to Christianity and the Jewish "superstitions" implied in it indicate the beginning of a new search for religious values coloured, however, by strong racial prejudices (Aronson Ibid p. 97).

For, according to Schopenhauer, Christianity was essentially an upshoot of the Jewish religion, and he was neither the first nor the last in the history of German scholarship to resent the semitic imposition on the cultural and religious life of the Aryans.

Hegel, Goethe, Gobineau, Nietzsche, Max Weber, Schiller can, therefore, be called the chief architects of the nazi philosophy borrowing heavily from Brahminism. They spoke about the "White principle", "superiority of the West", and "the superman as distinguished from the herd".

> "Metaphorically speaking, it was the Indian Brahmins who first of all enunciated the ideal of the superman",

says Alex Aronson (Ibid p. 102). The superman or the *guru* wants implicit obedience of the herd. Nietzsche has nothing but all praise for such a social system — superiority of a master caste (Brahmins) over all other castes. His book, *Thus Spake Zarathustra*, constitutes his final judgement of things Eastern.

Survival of the fittest

German writers intoxicated by the Brahmin literature started rejecting all other established thoughts and started asserting the German superiority. German, not Latin, was called the original language of Europe. Hebrew is derived from German language. Such myths were built up as a precursor to the Aryan myth. (Poliakov Ibid. p.96). The principal builder of the Aryan myth was Frederich Schlegel. The quintessence of his philosophy was that Germans were Aryans and a "chosen people" born to rule the world. Aryans originated in Germany and later migrated to India. Such fantastic theories were sold.

Every other language was denounced and the cult of German language was built up and a quest for "German religion" began. Germans were claimed to be superior to the Romans. Leon Poliakov speaking about this German madness says such "conclusions were based on a pride which tended to barbarism". (Ibid p.98).

The theory of the "survival of the fittest", supposed to have been formulated by Darwin and perfected later by Herbert Spencer, is again derived from the *Vedic* ideas manufactured by the Brahmins. So too Hitler's maxim of "Guns before butter".

If we go through these Vedic scriptures, the one single central idea sold there is that nobody can directly worship the god without a priest and that priest shall be the Brahmin and a Brahmin alone is declared as the chosen representative of the god. Nay, the god himself. So the godhood is conferred on the Brahmin by the Brahmin himself. The Brahmin thus becomes the thief, the police, the prosecutor, the judge, the jailor and the hangman.

Darwin, who divided the human species into superior and inferior races, was profoundly influenced by the "chosen people" theory propounded in the Aryan scriptures. Darwin's cousin, Francis Galton (1822-1911), improved upon the "science of eugenics" to "show that mental characteristics, and primarily intelligence, were hereditary in the same way as physical qualities." (Leon Poliakov, *Aryan Myth* p.292). The Whites alone were genius but the Blacks worthless, fit to be slaves.

Merit & efficiency

Heredity is again hailed as the sheet anchor of the Brahmin philosophy followed even to this day in India. The "reservations" (affirmative action) to Untouchables, Tribals and Backward Castes is meeting with stiff opposition from the Brahmins who argue that "merit" will suffer if the "low castes" occupy important positions. "Efficiency and Merit", therefore, are seen as hereditary characteristics of the "high-born" Hindu. The vast masses of India, comprising over 85% of its population, are today suffering racial discrimination because of this Aryan Myth of meritocracy. Darwin, Spencer, Freud, Kant, Earnest Heeckel, Drumont, Jung — all these scholars propounded their theories mainly inspired by this Aryan myth of meritocracy.

The Brahmins of India say that "free competition" should be

allowed, meaning the weak should be trampled upon. To them the American model of capitalist system is ideal.

House of Krupps & Birlas

The German Nazis greeted this "theory of natural selection" with enthusiasm because that was the only way to keep the Jews out. Darwinism was thus used for an anti-Semitic propaganda. The theory of "race hygiene" suited the German capitalists and the House of Krupps financed it, says Poliakov (Ibid p.294). In India, the Birlas financed Brahminism under the leadership of the fellow Bania, M.K. Gandhi.

The Aryans are even now criticising the Indian Constitution for not prescribing a qualification for the voters. The principle of one man one vote has sounded the death knell of the Aryans. Therefore, they are wanting to introduce the "merit theory" to the voters as well. Darwin who became the supreme authority for militarists the world over by propounding the "survival of the fittest", which in other words means "might is right", is thus a creature of the Ayan myth.

Muslim "invaders"

See the worldwide ramifications of the Aryan tyranny. Therefore, we have been often arguing that Brahminism is not a religion but a deadly ideology of oppression. And a menace to the whole world.

A German diplomat, Wilhem von Pochh Ammer, who considered India as a "second homeland", has given lot of evidence of the German sympathy for the Indian Aryans. And it is no wonder a Brahmin journalist reviewing (*Indian Express* March 7, 1982) his book, *India's Road to Nationhood* (Allied Publishers, Bombay pp. 678, Rs. 125) is all praise for the Germans. The German author pays high tributes to Brahmins for "protecting" the Indian culture from the "Muslim invaders" and, therefore, he describes Brahmins as the protectors of Indian culture. The author lists several "Indian revolutionaries" and almost all of them are Brahmins. Savarkar is hailed as one such revolutionary.

Albert Schweitzer verdict

Nietzsche, who is so popular with Brahmins who used his thoughts to defend their racist and fascist thoughts, is the chief inspiration for the current social conflict in the world and India in particular.

> "What is ripe for death should be allowed to die and should not be sustained, rather those who are falling should be struck down so that they fall the more quickly, for is anything worse (said *Zarathustra*) than degeneration?"

Nietzsche's hate philosophy suited the German nazis to single out the Jews for attack because "he seemed to assign the first place to the Jews". (Poliakov Ibid p.300).

Albert Schweitzer was the lone German philosopher who refused to be deceived by the theory of Aryan myth and refused to acknowledge the Aryans as the ancestors of Germany. He said the brahminical literature was devoid of ethics, in a devastating judgement. He condemned the Aryan theory which assigned the superman-status to Brahmins and inflicted apartheid upon the Untouchables. (*Indian Thought and its Development*, 1980, Wilco Publishers, 33-Ropewalk Lane, Rampart Row, Bombay-1). He said:

> "Brahmans showed no interest in the higher development of the religion of the people. They were not pre-occupied with ethics" (p.28). The Brahmins preached renunciation of the world to others while themselves leading a life of eternal pleasure (p.39). He also points out that the much-publicised non-violence is not part of the brahminical religion (p. 80). In fact war and violence, reckless killing, which is the present-day scene in India, has full religious sanction under Brahminism, says the world famous Nobel laureate (p.189).

This is also the central message of the *Gita* in which God Krishna himself gives the order to Arjuna to murder.

Germans hail *Gita*

But unfortunately it is this very *Gita* that was welcomed with great enthusiasm in Germany. William Von Humbolt praised the *Gita*, and wrote a letter to Fr. Von Gentz (1827) saying:

> "It is probably the most profound and most sublime work the world can show" (Ibid p.190).

But Scheweitzer warns us that the *Gita* marks the victory of Brahmins over Budhism.

But the wonder of all wonders is that the world's different philosophers, social scientists and historians who have produced mountains of literature on fascism, nazism and racism could not make out that Brahminism is the mother of all the three. Nor did they even list Brahminism under nazism. To that extent the mother of nazism has hid itself from even scholarly eyes. That is its greatness.

Today, it is a fashion to call every dictator a fascist but to this day the world is ignorant of the fact that India's brahminical thought is a fascist thought despite the fact that India practices the world's worst form of apartheid. And exploitation exists here in its most naked form.

Jews as victims of Brahminism

Jews unfortunately became the first victims of Brahminism outside India. Some years ago when we called the Brahmins as the "Jews of India", the noted French historian who is also a Jew, Dr. Leon Poliakov, wrote a letter (*Dalit Voice* Nov.16, 1983) saying that we had committed a great historical blunder in using such a name. He said the Jews were the victims of nazism which was built out of the philosophy of Brahminism. Brahminism being the chief inspiration for the killers of Jews, they cannot be called the "Jews of India". He said Jews were always hated, victimised and killed by others. Jews never killed anybody. How could the victims of Brahminism be dubbed brahminical?

Brahminism, he said, always stood for violence and oppressed those who did not subscribe to the Brahminical Social Order.

> "Please do not insult the Jews, who have produced many thinkers, scholars and scientists, by calling the Indian Brahmins as the Jews of India", he said.

We immediately apologised and stopped using this expression. We sent the apology through Mrs. Yumi Tsuji, our friend in Japan who introduced Dr. Leon Poliakov to us. Our book, *Who is the Mother of Hitler,* (Dalit Sahitya Akademy - 1984) was dedicated to Sister Yumi.

But what happened later?

Palestine and zionism

Hitler died and the Second World War ended. And the victorious White Western rulers allowed the zionists to annex the Muslim territory of Palestine and handed it over to Jews.

From that day India's Hindu nazis became the greatest admirers of zionism. **(See Annexure 1&2).**

The very people who once inspired the nazis to kill the Jews became the closest allies of Jews.

Zionist-Brahmin axis directing US

India's ruling Brahminical Social Order (BSO) recognised Israel brushing all opposition from India's huge Muslim population and also Muslim countries outside. And as this is written the zionists and India's Brahmins have become so close as to guide if not direct the US, the world's sole super power, in its anti-terrorist (read Muslim) war and violence. The Sept.11, 2001 "terrorist" attack on America is said to be a zionist conspiracy to bring about a clash between the Christian and Muslim worlds. India's ruling BSO is taking a prominent international role in its war against Muslims and Islam in full cooperation and collaboration with zionists who control the entire US Government, its economy and media. The US does not care for the United Nations and has no concern for human rights. The brahminical-zionist axis has been firmly established, proving itself to be poised for world domination.

The zionists came to India in a big way in the guise of the New World Order (NWO) of President Bush (senior). And the Hindu nazis of India embraced the NWO because it is the latest shape and name taken by the discredited Brahminism or nazism. We don't know what Dr. Leon Poliakov (who died in 1997) and Mrs. Yumi Tsuji will have to say on this metamorphosis of Brahminism.

America as the Big Satan

And that is how we declare that Brahminism has now become a global problem. What is the basis of our argument that Brahminism has become an international problem?

Today, the biggest threat to world peace is America which is leading the entire White Western world. It is this American ruling class that engineered the Gulf War (1991). It is the US that caused the break-up of Soviet Russia. It is the US that is acting as the policeman of the world. It is America that is beating the war drums against Muslims and Islam with the reckless bombing of Afghanistan in 2001 and vowing to continue the war against Iran and Iraq. It is again America that is backing the Zionist Israeli Prime Minister Ariel Sharon to exterminate Palestine after eliminating Yasser Arafat. (For details read American intellectual Naom Chomsky's lectures in India, *Frontline* Magazine, Dec.21, 2001).

Soviet Russia has been the only support for the Third World. After the death of the USSR, America has emerged as the sole super power. And behaving as if it is the owner of the whole world.

And this super power — the Big Satan — is guided by the zionists.

And this unholy alliance of racism, imperialism, colonialism, capitalism is in league with zionism.

And this combined might of racism, capitalism and zionism, guided by the brahminical hate philosophy, has come to India in a big way to help the ruling Brahminical Social Order to crush the 85% non-Hindus.

White Western racism, zionism and Brahminism, this triangle of tyrants facing the world, are on the rampage as this is written. Their immediate target is Islam. Then the Blacks and then the Yellows (China). But will this mad bull have a free run? Will the saner people of the world allow it to trample all of us?

Muslims as the principal enemy

Today, all these people have only one principal enemy — that is Muslims. (DV Editorial March 16, 1992: "*Why the whole world hates Muslims and Islam?*"). But in many parts of the world Muslims and Blacks are the same.

The world today is divided into two neat camps: (1) Imperialism, racism, zionism, Brahminism - on one side and (2) those opposed to it on the other side: Muslims, Blacks, India's Black Untouchables and Yellows (China).

Third World War

If the "Big Satan" rushes at the present speed the Third World War will come about as a clash between the two camps. And in this war, the first is bound to be defeated.

Following the Sept.11, 2001 "terrorist" attack on America, the US Government, goaded by the zionist forces, launched a deadly war on Afghanistan to catch Osama bin Laden, the alleged "mastermind" behind the attack and a Saudi billionaire, but President George Bush, who vowed to catch Osama "dead or alive", could not even locate him till the time of writing this. Nor could he catch the Afghan Taliban chief Mulla Omar. The US might have destroyed the whole of

Afghanistan by raining more bombs than what was used in the II World War. But the purpose of launching the war (2001) was defeated as the two "culprits" could not be caught but the US and its drum-beaters including India's rulers are claiming victory in Afghanistan. After having "defeated" Afghanistan, the US under pressure from zionists decided to expand the war against the "axis of evil" — Iran, Iraq and North Korea. The above US decision announced in the State of the Union speech by President George W. Bush on Jan.29, 2002 should make it clear even to a child that the US under total zionist control is all-out to finish Islam and Muslims and then go to eliminate the Yellows (China) through North Korea. Combined with the explosive scene developing in West Asia on the Palestine front, the latest postures of the US is nothing but a preparation to launch the Third World War.

Fascism's Indian ancestry

That is why we say that Brahminism is not merely the enemy of India but the enemy of the whole world. That is why we use the word "nazi" to call all those who subscribe to Brahminism because the roots of fascism and nazism are found in Brahminism.

Some honest Germans are offended by our use of the word "nazi" to denote the brahminical forces. They wrote saying our use of the word nazi revived memories of Hitler's Germany. But just because certain things are unpleasant to our friends in Germany, we cannot bury history. And history says Brahminism is the mother of nazism.

The Rashtriya Swayamsevak Sangh (RSS), the chief Hindu nazi organisation of India, openly propagates caste dictatorship. Hitler and Mussolini, the world's most famous dictators, got their inspiration from Brahminism based on the dangerous philosophy of *karma* which asks the "poor" to bear their poverty with a smile and resign to their fate. Brahminism seeks unquestioned obedience. (*Gita* IV-39-40). *Gita* was the guide for M.K. Gandhi and to the whole Hindus.

M.N. Roy, the founder of the Indian Communist Party, in his book, *Fascism* (Jijnasa, 133/A, Rasbehari Avenue, Calcutta-29, 1938), says the philosophy of fascism was inspired by the Aryan spirit of caste system.

> "Fascism's Indian ancestry can be traced through Schopenhauer whose disciple, Nietzsche, was the father of the philosophy of Fascism", says Roy (Ibid p.13).

So, we repeat that Brahminism is the mother of fascism, nazism, racism.

The German nazis may be dead but the Aryan nazis who supplied the deadly philosophy to nazis, are still alive and going strong — spreading their tentacles to the whole world. That means Brahminism has not only enslaved Indians, including Brahmins, but it is creating problems to the whole world.

Leon Poliakov had once said that even Jews were victims of Brahminism. But today, Jews have joined hands with the brahminical rulers of India. The clock has turned the full circle.

VI- Anti-Brahminism as an Ideology

Anti-Brahminism may not be a perfect, systematic ideology but it undoubtedly is a powerful philosophy which once moved and still moves millions of people not only among Hindus in India but others as well. Since some urban-bred people cannot so much appreciate the importance and significance of this most powerful indigenous ideology, an effort is being made here to go into its different aspects.

How anti-Brahminism, a negative concept, can be an ideology, a philosophy? It is being described so for want of any other appropriate name. When Brahminism can be called a philosophy, why not anti-Brahminism? Suffice it to say that the revolt against the domination of Brahmins, and even those non-Brahmins immediately below them in the Hindu caste hierarchy, by those who have suffered at the hands of Brahminism has played and continues to play a great role in shaping the Indian society and politics. Anti-Brahminism has been, therefore, the central theme of all protest movements in India from centuries — from the days the Aryans invaded India.

Three pillars of Brahminism

However, anti-Brahminism cannot be confined merely to a revolt against the Brahmins alone but all those non-Brahmins also who subscribe to their value system. Brahminism is, therefore, more dangerous than Brahmins. Because, the Brahmins themselves have been the victims of Brahminism. From the Budha, the greatest enemy of Brahminism, Basaveshwara, Guru Nanak, Raja Ram Mohan Roy, Dayananda Saraswati, to Mahatma Phule, Narayana Guru, Dr. Ambedkar, R.M. Lohia and Periyar E.V. Ramaswamy — all of them rank among India's most virulent crusaders against Brahminism.

Therefore, anti-Brahminism is considered the most indigenous among the different secular ideologies of India. Social or political leaders can ignore this ideology only at their peril. What gives teeth to anti-Brahminism is the caste system which is a specific Indian phenomenon. Caste is the curse of Hinduism with its ascending order of reverence and descending degree of contempt. Anti-Brahminism believes that the caste structure with the Brahmin standing at the apex of this deathless pyramid is the root cause of exploitation, inhumanity and slavery in India. The Brahmin domination has the religious sanction and the Brahmin hereditary priesthood plays the central role in perpetuating Brahminism. So, anti-Brahminism calls for destruction of its three major institutions — the Sacred Scriptures, the caste system and the priestcraft. This is the quintessence of its philosophy. Including the Brahmin, every Hindu has been the victim of Brahminism, particularly the Untouchables many of whom have sought refuge in other liberating religions to escape its tyranny. Women, including Brahmin women, have suffered silently from the barbarity of Brahminism. Even Vivekananda and Gandhi, two of its greatest pillars, were forced to speak out against the havoc caused by Brahminism. M.N. Roy and Jawaharlal Nehru, both Brahmins, had also lent powerful support to anti-Brahminism. Democracy and caste system cannot coexist, they said.

Father of anti-Brahminism

Anti-Brahminism has thus become the most powerful ideology that did not fail to move a single social, cultural, literary and political movement in India from the days of Jainism, over 2,500 years ago. Every political party was rocked by it. Even the communist parties are not spared and many splits have taken place because of the Indian marxist refusal to heed the pulls of this ideology.

Mahatma Phule of Maharashtra is considered the father of this anti-Brahminism in recent times. Author of several books on this philosophy and the founder of the powerful Satya Shodak Movement, he described *Manusmriti* as an unholy book. Dr. B.R. Ambedkar, an Untouchable, was mainly inspired by Phule who belonged to a (gardener) Backward Caste.

Anti-Brahminism also became the ideology of a powerful social, cultural and political movement for realising the Dravidian identity of Tamils. Founded in 1944 by Periyar E.V. Ramaswamy, the DMK of Annadurai came as an offshoot of Dravida Kazagham (DK) in 1949. Periyar improved upon this philosophy and ridiculed the Hindu gods and the Hindu religion itself. Hinduism, he said, is founded by Brahmins to exploit the poor, illiterate, ignorant masses. The abolition of Brahmin priestly services was his basic programme. Dr. Ambedkar follows a similar line of thinking. He says the caste deadens, paralyses and cripples the people. It has ruined the Hindus and has destroyed, demoralised and devitalised the Hindu society. Ranked as the greatest thinker and philosopher of modern India, Dr. Ambedkar in his innumerable books has given a call to free every woman and man from the thraldom of Sacred Scriptures. He also considers the priest as the real villain of Brahminism. Both Dr. Ambedkar and Periyar have dubbed Brahminism as a reactionary philosophy.

Foreigners in Tamil Nadu

What did anti-Brahminism achieve? By reviving the glorious cultural and social traditions of the original inhabitants of India existing before the Aryan invasion, it helped them to find their roots, get a self-identity, a self-respect. Phule, Dr. Ambedkar and Periyar said the *shudras* and the *ati-shudras* (Untouchables) with Tribals were the original inhabitants of India before the Aryan invasion. They produced enough historical evidences. To condemn the Brahmin as a foreigner in Tamil Nadu has become a handy weapon of the non-Brahmin to beat the Brahmin with, but the popularising of the myth of their Dravidian origin also gave to the Tamil non-Brahmins both an identity and a self-confidence, says E.F. Irshick. Evidences have also been found to prove that the Tamil country was free from idol-worship and caste system before Brahminism invaded.

Persecution of Jains & Budhists

The Indus Valley Civilisation has conclusively proved that the Aryans were not the first or the most important creators of Indian culture. Father Heras said that Tamils were the purest cultural descendants of the Indus Valley. Brahminism being a proseletysing religion it savagely persecuted Jains and Budhists and reconverted them to Hinduism, a new name given to Brahminism after the death of the Budha. Murder and torture of Budhists and Jains is cited by many historians. Behind the DK-DMK slogan of "Tamil for Tamilians" lies the conviction that Aryans are the aliens and non-Brahmins are the Dravidians. Anti-Brahminism has thus brought a new awakening, a new pride among the non-Brahmins and convinced them that their deprivation, poverty and suffering were due to Brahminism. The emphasis given to social revolution has made them conscious of their exploitation at the hands of Brahmins.

Manuwadi marxists

So much so, many non-Brahmins preferred the British rule to Brahmin rule. Both Dr. Ambedkar and Periyar EVR boldly said so. It is this anti-Brahminism that drove Periyar out of the Congress Party and made him found the Self-Respect Movement. Later, he launched an agitation for separate Dravidastan. Periyar also said the so-called nationalism is nothing but Brahminism in another form. The growth of RSS, Jan Sangh (now BJP) has confirmed their fears. Lohia has contributed a great deal to the promotion of anti-Brahminism in the Hindu heartland. Lohiaites all over India are today in the vanguard of anti-Brahminism.

It is to be noted that all the leaders of anti-Brahminism came into conflict with the Indian Left movement for ignoring the basic principles of its philosophy. All of them warned that marxism, an alien philosophy, cannot take roots in India as long as it fails to attack Brahminism and its three pillars. Dr. Ambedkar said Brahminism and capitalism are the twin enemies of the working class and thus both must be attacked simultaneously. He criticised S.A. Dange, the lone Lenin Order winner in India, and others controlling the communist parties as a "bunch of Brahmin boys". Periyar was also critical of the Brahmin domination of the communist parties. So too Lohia.

Brahmins driven out of political power

Caste being the principal contradiction in India, its elimination should be our prime effort. One of the greatest impacts of anti-Brahminism was on education. Phule and Dr. Ambedkar launched an education drive among the "low castes" laying stress on anti-Brahminism in their books. Dr. Ambedkar has set up a chain of educational institutions. Both Phule and Periyar introduced anti-Brahmin interpretation to the *Puranas*— the *Ramayana* and *Mahabharata*, the epics, and interpreted them as a fight between Brahmins and non-Brahmins. Bonfires of the *Gita* and *Manusmriti*, which spread the poison of Brahminism, became popular. Dr. Ambedkar himself publicly burnt the *Manusmriti* in 1927. Periyar entered temples and broke idols, burnt scriptures, tarred hotel name boards bearing Brahmin names, cut Brahmin tufts. His most popular programme which turned out to be a mass movement is the "self-respect marriage", which eliminates priests. He also established a powerful press and a publishing house at Madras. Periyar will thus go down in the history of India as one of the greatest pillars of anti-Brahminism. Unfortunately, his rationalist crusades got confined to Tamil Nadu as he was not good at English or other languages.

The inspiration behind anti-Brahminism is the search for justice, equality and human respect. The non-Brahmins might not have secured these to their satisfaction but certainly they have at least succeeded in driving the Brahmins out of political power. Dr. Ambedkar did not reject religion as such. He went over to Budhism. But Periyar was a militant atheist. To him conversion was no solution. Periyar called for the destruction of Hinduism. Therefore, he is rightly hailed as India's first and foremost rationalist who was able to win over people of all castes including the Untouchables. However, his followers later started compromising, forced by their greed for political power and thus gradually played into the hands of Brahmins. Periyar had strictly warned that the Dravidian movement must be confined to cultural and social issues and should not stray into electoral politics. The followers did not heed this advice and as a result they lost the battle in their war against Brahminism and handed over Tamil Nadu back to Brahmins.

No other ideology has helped the submerged sections of India as much as anti-Brahminism. If the masses in South India are better informed, more progressive and militant than their counterparts in the North, the credit must go to this ideology. It had its impact on all other ideologies including marxism. India's topmost marxist, the late E.M.S. Namboodiripad, has admitted this in an article in the *Economic & Political Weekly* (Feb.1979).

Shudras join Brahmins

Unfortunately, anti-Brahminism started losing its teeth in recent times because all those non-Brahmins who climbed up the ladder of life with the help of this ideology deserted, if not betrayed, the movement and joined the enemy camp— thanks to the brahminical trap of sanskritization and westernization. The upper caste non-Brahmins particularly those belonging to the landed *shudra* castes turned into neo-

Brahmins if not super Brahmins and thus swelled the ranks of Brahminism. Not only these beneficiaries of anti-Brahminism have been indifferent to the plight of the more oppressed group lower below the caste ladder, particularly the Untouchables, but more than that they have turned out to be the fighting arm of the Brahmins. The best example in the country is that of Shudra Kayasth, Bal Thackeray, who is posing as a super Hindu nazi. So much so the Brahmins have started telling the Untouchables that it is not they who are committing atrocities on them but the non-Brahmins. These are the very non-Brahmin oppressors who were once in the forefront of the anti-Brahmin movement to displace the Brahmins from positions of power. Once they occupied it after driving out the Brahmins, they started imitating the Brahmins and excelled them in cruelty. If the army of the oppressed should not suffer defection and desertion and if it has to gain strength day by day, the purest indigenous ideology of anti-Brahminism will have to be suitably amended to combine class struggle, the marxian concept, with "caste struggle". A happy welding of marxism with anti-Brahminism, which we had described as "class-caste struggle" or "Indian Marxism", can alone bring us the desired result.

(*Dalit Voice* Editorial Sept.16, 1983).

VII - Brahmin as a Sociological Wonder

The Brahmins of India like the Jews have always been an enigma. The mystique of Brahmin's survival, his identity and his solidarity have aroused the wonder, sometimes the jealousy and often the ire of generations and generations.

Aspects of this strange phenomenon are questioned not only by the so-called non-Brahmins but Brahmins themselves have lately been in a bitter conflict between themselves torn between tradition and modernity, between revivalism and socialism. The very Brahmin value system has faced numerous crises down the ages and yet it has survived, every time re-emerging with redoubled glory. A wonder of wonders — India's greatest wonder.

As India's ruling class

No doubt, the very uniqueness of the brahminical experience has turned mystery into suspicion and incomprehension into hostility. Brahmins just cannot be slotted neatly into any past or existing category of human grouping. They are neither simply a "*varna*" nor a race, nor a community. They are a singular amalgam of all the three — the undoubted, the unquestioned aristocrats of India. Dr. Babasaheb B.R. Ambedkar, India's greatest social scientist and an authority on Brahmins and Brahminism, called them India's ruling class.

Unlike other undefinable Hindus of India — all part of this ageless, deathless, hierarchical caste pyramid — Brahmins are the only section that has preserved its identity since antiquity even without a common territory, wonderously surviving by the sheer dint of their supreme strategies and tactics facing all sorts of hostility, shuffling *varnas*, dividing every other caste and subcaste, sometimes promoting a lower caste into a higher one, while maintaining a solid unity all through the history. Never has the country seen one section of the Brahmins joining hands with some others to fight any hostile Brahmin force.

We may have a Subramaniam Swamy criticising an Atal Behari Vajpayee but when it comes to the question of fighting the forces hostile, the Brahmins forget all their internal differences and collectively fight the rest. Such a solidarity is unparalleled in the world. That is why as a community they survived every crisis unlike the Jews who allegedly had to face extermination under Hitler.

A nation within nation

A nation within a nation, Brahmins are the only people in the subcontinent jealously guarding a civilisation, upholding that "divine language", Sanskrit, against successive onslaughts and professing the same religion as they did 3,000 years ago, devouring every other protest movement including the most virulent Budhism that came in its way.

Again, there is clearly something quite amazingly uncommon in a numerically insignificant people (forming about 3% of the total population of India) who have registered such a high rating in the "honours list" for spiritual, cultural, literary, educational, scientific, social, economic and political achievements and who continue to feature so centrally in all national and international affairs. Of the 12 Prime Ministers that "independent" India had seen, seven were Brahmins.

India is thus synonymous with Brahmin. Brahmin is India and India is Brahmin. Minus the Brahmin, India will be an impoverished lot, a big cypher. Its history is the history of Brahmins, its culture is the culture of Brahmins, its achievement is the achievement of Brahmins. To that extent they have so jealously guarded and preserved everything for themselves leaving the rest so culturally deprived.

Gods on earth

Historians, both Indian and foreign, have admitted their centuries of supremacy — leaders of the people, custodians of religions and secular learning, unrivalled captains of every walk of life, owners of wealth and power, besides being the trustees of the people's conscience as priests. Probably no other class of people in any society in the world ever combined so effectively in themselves all these multi-faceted glories, such all-embracing powers so exclusively as the Brahmins. The much publicised "glorious cultural heritage" of India is the achievements of Brahmins being the custodians of culture.

> "*Devadhinam jagat sarvam,*
> *Mantradhinam ta devata*
> *Tan Mantram brahmanadhinam*
> *Brahmana mama devata*"

(The universe is under the power of the gods; the gods are under the power of the *mantras*, the *mantras* are under the power of the Brahmins, therefore, the Brahmins are our gods).

Hence they fully deserve the sublime title of *Bhoodevatas* or Gods of the Earth. (V.T. Rajshekar: *Dialogue of Bhoodevatas*, Dalit Sahitya Akademy - 1993).

Supreme among the more tangible factors accounting for this phenomenon is the highly developed sense of solidarity among the Brahmins expressed in the remarkable stability and "togetherness" of brahminical life, no less than in the profound concern of Brahmin communities everywhere for each others' welfare and security.

Offence better than defence

For others, this feeling of togetherness and inter-dependence may seem unduly clannish; for Brahmins it is indispensable for their survival. Offence is the best form of defence. For others it may be difficult to understand why Brahmins in far-off Tamil Nadu continually demonstrate for the welfare of their brethren in Kashmir thousands of miles away.

That is why Periyar E.V. Ramaswamy, India's bitterest critic of Brahmins, once said:

"If it rains in Kashmir, Brahmins in Kanyakumari will catch cold".

To that extent they think alike and act alike from Kashmir to Kanyakumari length-wise, from Gujarat to Assam breadth-wise. Partly, of course, the strength of brahminical solidarity like that of the Jews has been forged by adversity. As necessity is the mother of invention, so the need to triumph over common suffering bigots the fellowship of united resistance. The once uncrowned king of India is today thrown into open competition with the other Wretched of the Earth and made to do even manual work for his survival. The Brahmins have come to know that in this mad race for the crumbs of government under a Constitution committed to reservation (affirmative action) they are driven to the wall being a numerical minority.

To the Brahmin, the future is bleak. His heart breaks as he sees with his own eyes the collapse of the very edifice he so laboriously built and enjoyed it through and through.

To the Brahmins, therefore, the unity is never before so important and urgent as it is today for self-preservation, self-defence. Naturally, his heart goes to the "poor" among Brahmins. And there are any number of "poor Brahmins" despite all their proximity to god and their Sacred Scriptures.

As masters of the law of contradictions, (Mao Tse-tung: *On Contradiction*, Foreign Languages Press, Peking-1967) they have been effectively managing —putting one man against the other through their favourite game of divide and rule.

Simple living and high thinking is the hallmark of a Brahmin. A Brahmin household is the personification of simplicity and cleanliness. Essentially a vegetarian barring West Bengal and Kashmir, a Brahmin lives on leaves and roots and by such frugal habits — a life noted for its stark discipline, study, prayer, dedication and sacrifice shunning all pomp, pleasure and show. The Brahmin is not afraid of the chill penury of poverty because he has lived with it.

Brahmin as a poor man

In fact, a Brahmin is always pictured as a poor man. Textbooks have innumerable references to a "poor Brahmin". These books will never say that there was a Brahmin but always speak about a "poor Brahmin". To that extent poverty is made to be associated with the Brahmins. Textbook writers have successfully projected the image of a Brahmin as poor man. Poverty and Brahmins go together. No other section in the country is so caste-conscious as the Brahmins. Justice V.R. Krishna Iyer of the Supreme Court says:

> "the *Harijan*, the *bhangi*, does not have a dog's chance of equality with the Brahmin as the political power in India is still caste conscious." (*Statesman* Dec.18, 1976).

They are the only people in India having a genuine feeling for the "poor" among them. While "caste feeling" exists among all other *jatis*, Brahmins both rich and poor are the only people who speak with one voice and stand like one man. However much poverty-stricken or exploited, a "poor Brahmin" is not ready to fight a rich Brahmin if ever a "class war" develops in India. To that extent they think alike and act alike — with rhythmic precision. The well-to-do among them never keep aloof from the "poor Brahmins". The rich Brahmin's heart bleeds for the poor among them —the "poor *archaka*", the cook, the school teacher.

Caste-based reservation

They are worried that caste-based reservations will seriously jeopardise their position. Hence with a tremendous foresight they have successfully made the country accept the "poverty yardstick" based on their "merit" mantra. They have convinced a large section of the society that caste-based reservation will affect "merit and efficiency". And there is a chorus for it. And that is the greatness of Brahmin ingenuity and its universal acceptability. To that extent the Brahmin has conditioned the country's mind. Nay. The brain of every Indian is kept in the Brahmin fridge.

Apparently, the "poor Brahmins" are never sorry about their pitiable state of affairs. Their poverty is nothing for them in the face of the supreme consolation of belonging to the highest strata of Hindu hierarchy, the apex of the caste pyramid. The supreme position enjoyed by them has so blinded the "poor Brahmins" that they refuse to see the irrelevance of the caste gradations on a hereditary basis. The late Jagjivan Ram might have been the Deputy Prime Minister and "India's richest politician", but when he unveiled the statue of Dr. Sampoornanand at the Varanasi Sanskrit University, even the "poor" Brahmin boys joined in cleansing the statue with *Ganga jal* to purify it from pollution. The "poor Brahmins" are therefore more caste-conscious than the rich Brahmins who with wealth may acquire a streak of cosmopolitan outlook.

The extraordinary cohesion of the Brahmins in their widely scattered dispersion is largely also the product of their religious nurture and priestcraft, so well preserved even to this day in the millions of temples that dot the length and breadth of India. A striking example is the concept of corporate responsibility among Brahmins and its impact on Brahmin solidarity. As the Talmud put it nearly 2,000 years ago: "All Jews are accountable for each other". This is true of the Brahmins Diaspora also. As an extension of this concept, the Brahmin brain has been conditioned to regard Brahminism as the highest ideal, and its profanation as the worst offence.

M.N. Roy case

When a Brahmin acts disreputably, he is privately cursed for having disgraced the Brahmin community. Conversely, if he distinguishes himself by some special noble act, all Brahmins share in his glory and praise him sky-high through all the media and platform at their command that the rest of the population is stunned, mystified, overawed, demoralised and finally silenced and made to humbly submit and surrender. Another great Brahmin quality is never to let down a fellow-Brahmin. Whatever a Brahmin does is admired and broadcast in the loudest voice. Whatever he does is right. If a Brahmin rebels (example M.N. Roy) against his own community, he is praised for being non-communal. He is admired for his "broad-mindedness". But this concession is not extended to a non-Brahmin like Dr. R.M. Lohia who was ridiculed as a buffoon.

A Brahmin can be a marxist, communist, maoist, athiest, anarchist, revivalist, fascist, naxalite. He can be anti-Brahmin, anti-god, anti-socialist and anti-human and still he is lauded and paraded. But a non-Brahmin is not given this freedom, this luxury. He simply cannot survive in India if once he is dubbed an "anti-Brahmin". Even non-Brahmins hate an anti-Brahmin. This is the greatness of his *sanatana dharma*. Since everybody tries to imitate the ruling class, the Brahmin has become the symbol of perfection — a paragon of all virtues. He is not to be blamed for it. The "lower castes" in their relentless bid for *sanskritisation*, want to climb up the caste ladder and some how reach the coveted summit — a place originally reserved for the Brahmin. Hence, he is the ideal.

Dalits imitating Brahmins

Many Dalits have taken to Brahmin surname of Sharma. Millions are climbing this ladder and dreaming of reaching their cherished goal and if one stray, solitary, discordant voice like Dr. B.R. Ambedkar tries to tell them not to climb, not to aim at that summit, not to fall a prey to blind imitation — the national rat race — it is but natural that the rest get furious.

Brahminism has thus become the other name for elitism. The elite —the English-speaking affluent class — may be numerically small. But it is the most influential class forming the top 15% of the country's population. It may belong to diverse castes and communities but all of them subscribe to the same brahminical thought process. An increase in the number of elites, through the twin process of sanskritisation and westernisation, will indirectly strengthen Brahminism. And this is bound to happen as English education spreads among the lower castes.

Exclusive club

Brahminism thus does not confine to Brahmins alone. It is the other name for a group of people subscribing to a particular thought process that helps them to join this exclusive club. Brahminism, therefore, is not confined to the Brahmin community alone, though the Brahmins are its foremost champions and its most important promulgators. Brahminism, therefore, does not signify Brahmins alone but an ancient order of things of which the Brahmins are only the leaders and champions. The twin effect of *sanskritisation* and westernisation will swell the ranks of the rulers. And Brahminism, therefore, has a glorious future in India.

The secret of the Brahmin invincibility is that he is the sole custodian of the god. Nobody can approach the god without him. The unique feature of Hinduism is that without the presence of the Brahmin nobody can get the blessings of god. Because the Brahmin is the god. Since he personifies the god, all Hindus and even non-Hindus are afraid of the Brahmin. This is the secret of the Brahmin power. Reject this Hindu god, the Brahmin is dead. Since every elite is corrupted and co-opted in Hindu India, he is afraid of the god, meaning the Brahmin — just as every thief is afraid of the police. The Brahmin is the policemen for all the thieves of India. Like the cockroach that feeds on the very poison that is meant to kill it and grows fat and fatter, Brahminism will use a very philosophy, every ideology, every strategy, every tactics, every contradiction meant to destroy Brahminism and grow fatter and fatter and prove to the world that Brahminism alone can lead people to success.

VIII - Brahminism as a Mental Disease Killing India

Keynote address delivered at the inauguration of the Bahujan Samaj, a new cultural organisation of Backward Caste /Dalit and Muslim intellectuals of Kerala on June 6, 1993 at Trichur, Kerala, South India.

Sub: "Brahminism, cause of India's backwardness".

Sisters and brothers,

I don't know what made you to select me to address a distinguished gathering of social scientists and intellectuals, that too on a subject on which I haven't had any specialization.

Except that I am a victim of Brahminism and also that I am the Editor of a journal dealing with India's vast "*Persecuted Nationalities Denied Human Rights*" — who are all victims of Brahminism — I have no other qualification.

Cultural capital

This is perhaps my second visit to Trichur. My earlier visit was on the invitation of the SNDP Yogam of the Backward Caste Ezhavas.

Normally, this subject of Brahminism is never discussed on public platforms. So much of secrecy surrounds this subject. Nobody has the courage particularly in recent years despite witnessing a tremendous upsurge in brahminical aggression.

That you made bold to discuss this subject at Trichur, the so-called cultural capital of Kerala, and that too in this very hall of the Kerala Sahitya Akademy, the centre of double-distilled Brahminism, proves that you are a set of people with courage and conviction.

Brahmin women

Though over 85% of India's population is the victim of Brahminism, including a section of Brahmins themselves and the entire lot of Brahmin women, very little discussion is taking place in this country in its press or platform. There is so much of fear. This was not so just 10-15 years ago. Periyar E.V. Ramaswamy used to publicly attack Brahminism. But today Tamil Nadu is under a Brahmin Chief Minister who has re-established the brahminical hegemony over the state.

This hesitation to discuss Brahminism in public is because the English-knowing people (a tiny, less than 2% of our population) and even the Indian language-knowing people are mostly from the upper castes who are benefited by Brahminism. This "educated class" has a vested interest in defending the Brahmin and Brahminism which is virtually controlling the entire world of property as well as the world of ideas.

Caste-ridden Kerala

And hence this "educated" section not only avoids any discussion on Brahminism but denigrates any writer or speaker who dares to touch this subject by dubbing him a casteist, communalist, hate-monger and hence anti-national.

Delhi's largest circulated English daily, Birla's *Hindustan Times*, now and then publishes my "Letters to Editor" in which I mildly criticise caste system and upper casteism. The moment my "Letter" is published some enraged but honest Brahmins directly write to me holding all sorts of threats. Of course, the "brave authors" of these letters don't write their names — not to speak of their addresses. They abuse me in the filthiest of language. This is the culture of the votaries of Brahminism. I pity them.

The point I am trying to make is no open discussion on Brahminism is allowed. When so much of secrecy is surrounding this subject your organisation has to be congratulated for openly announcing the subject matter of discussion and conducting an open debate on that. And that too in this caste-ridden "cultural capital" of Kerala.

Why this secrecy on this subject? It is because this delicate subject "hurts" our upper castes who are also the country's property-holders and hence rulers. The hundreds of Harshad Mehtas, who have acquired so much of illegal wealth with the help of Brahminism, will not like their dirty linen to be washed in public.

Nairs of Kerala

During the days of Swami Dharma Thirtha (Parameswara Menon), the author of the famous book, *History of Hindu Imperialism*, (Dalit Educational Literature Centre, PO Box 2296, Madras - 600 023, 1992 edition pp. 280), and a Nair, even non-Brahmins like the Nairs used to join us in critizing Brahminism.

An English book on the "Nairs of Kerala" refers to a Brahmin saying:

> "If ever a Nair were to become a university graduate, I will shave my mustache".

So much was the Brahmin-Nair hatred even as recently as 50 years ago. But today the same Nairs are the strongest advocates of Brahminism (*cheers*).

Such Nairs may be in the Congress or the marxist parties, naxalite parties or even the Kerala Sastra Sahitya Parishad but they all continue to be votaries of Brahminism.

Shudra muscle

This is because Brahminism has the tremendous capacity to co-opt its critics and make the new recruits to fight on behalf of Brahmins. Once upon a time *Vaidik* Brahmins were the sole sellers of Brahminism. When Vivekananda, a *shudra* (Kayasth), and then M.K. Gandhi, a Vaishya (Bania), jumped into the bandwagon of Brahmins, this Hindu nazi philosophy acquired a lot of respectability and muscle power. Today, the most vociferous practitioners of Brahminism are the *shudras* like the Nairs, Kayasths, Marathas, Vokkaligas, Lingayats, Reddys, Jats, Khammas.

Brahmins, of course, are there. There can be no Brahminism without the Brahmin. But being a cowardly lot, the Brahmins do not have the courage to engage the victims of Brahminism in a physical fight. This job is done by the *shudras*. The landed *shudras* have both the money and the muscle.

That is how in Karnatáka the two dominant landed *shudra* castes, Lingayats and Vokkaligas, Andhra Pradesh Reddys and Khammas have become the main oppressors of SC/ST/BCs and Muslims. And thereby they have become ardent upholders of Brahminism, which is getting new feathers, new vigour. This is the secret of the big jump in the popularity of our nazi parties like the RSS-BJP, Shiv Sena etc.

The subject you have given me is so vast (India's principal contradiction) that I cannot do justice to it even if you give me one whole day. But there is a time limit and we can discuss further when I answer questions.

Bal Thackeray example

One famous example can convince you how Brahminism is growing day by day and threatening the country's not only unity and integrity but also its social and economic well-being. The famous example is the Hindu Nazi Shiv Sena chief Bal Thackeray of Bombay. Today, this Thackeray is considered more brahminical than the pure brahminical party of Chitpavan Brahmins, namely the RSS.

Thackeray is a Kayasth who according to the Vedas are born out of *papayoni.*

His father, Prabhodankar Thakre, was the leader of the anti-Brahmin movement in Maharashtra before "independence". He even started a paper for his anti-Brahmin crusades. But what is his son doing? He is the greatest upholder of Brahminism, which is the father of racism, nazism, zionism.

The other example is the Dravidian leaders of Tamil Nadu —

both DMK and ADMK — born out of Periyar's virulent anti-Brahmin movement. How Bal Thackeray and the Tamil Nadu's Dravidian leaders transformed themselves into greatest bum-lickers of Brahmins?

The answer to this provides the key to the growth of Brahminism.

Corrupting & co-opting technique

Vaidik Brahminism or *Sanatana Dharma* first corrupts people through *sama* (reconciliation etc.) and *dana* (bribery etc.) and then *bedha* (creating ill-will, character assassination etc.). It resorts to *danda* (final punishment — killing) only when the first three weapons, used one after the other, fail. After corrupting a person it co-opts him and makes him a leader. After using him to the fullest extent, this leader is ditched. Throughout history we have had hundreds of such examples. Yet our people go on falling victim to the Brahmin net.

The Brahminical Social Order (BSO) has used all the three weapons against me but it did not succeed. So, the last weapon is reserved and may be used against me any time.

Crisis facing Ezhavas of Kerala

Such a corrupting technique was also used against the Ezhavas, the toddy tapper community of Kerala. Sri Narayana Guru was perhaps Kerala's most virulent crusader against Brahminism. "*Oru Matam, Oru Jati, Oru Daivam*" was his slogan. He installed the "Ezhava Shiva" who was not an Aryan god but a Dravidian deity. Shiva worshippers are in a big majority all over India. Hence to capture the Shiva *bhaktas*, a dwarf Namboodiri Brahmin from Kerala called Adi Shankara did the job of re-establishing Brahminism after destroying Budhism.

After this Adi Shankara, today you have the "Modern Shankara", E.M.S. Namboodiripad, to complete the job through marxism (laughter).

But the Guru's movement soon got corrupted and I witnessed

this corruption when I visited Varkala where I saw the Sanskrit word, *Om*, written all over and monks wearing *kavi* (saffron) dress, though the Guru wore a yellow robe. Nitya Chaitanya Yati has started giving discourses on the *Gita*, thereby once again pushing the once liberated Ezhavas back to slavery as *shudras* under Brahminism. Sri Narayana Guru had liberated the Ezhavas and constituted them into a separate community.

But this community, forming about 30% of the Kerala population — single largest community — got corrupted and that is how Brahminism was able to once again enslave and swallow them. The Guru never said that Ezhavas were Hindus. Like the Dalits, they are a separate entity. But today what happened to them? The "Modern Shankara", E.M.S.Namboodiripad, has made a mince-meat out of the Ezhavas.

Cross-thread marxists

Either under the Congress, the original brahminical party of India, or under the "Modern Shankara's" cross-thread marxist party, the Ezhavas could not get any justice.

Ezhavas are perhaps the country's best example of slaves enjoying their slavery. (*cheers*). Ezhavas did not have a single chief minister after R. Shankar though every party used them as its musclemen.

The upper castes fooled us in the name of marxism for 50 years. Marxism having failed, the cross-thread marxists have taken to new weapons to enslave us: environment and ecology. Trissur, I was told, is the centre for these fellows. Beware of these brahminical terrorists in the guise of ecology heroes - enemies of SC/ST/BCs, Muslims. (*cheers*).

Ezhavas are also a good example in the country to prove the efficacy of brahminical corrupting technique and how through corruption it enslaves a whole community. Do you know why the Ezhavas are enslaved? Because the Ezhavas have ceased to be an organized community. This is because the community lost its identity.

What do I mean when I say that you are no longer an organized group? Muslims, Christians, Sikhs are an organized community because they belong to an organized religion. But you (Ezhavas) say you are Hindus. Until you declare you are not Hindus and go back to the Guru and take shelter under his liberating religion, you will continue to suffer. The Guru never said that he was a Hindu.

The *Kerala Kaumudi*, the only Ezhava Malayalam daily, is having a Nair editor. To that extent your community is devoid of intellectual strength today. The SNDP Yogam must bend its head in shame.

Muslim League

Then we have the beautiful example of Kerala's Muslim League. Its leadership has been also corrupted by the BSO and that is why the oppressed Muslims are deserting the League. I was an eye-witness to the League leaders acting at the behest of the BSO when I went to inaugurate Brother Abdul Nasser Madani's new party, People's Democratic Party or PDP.

PDP is Kerala's party of the future. The brahminical press has tried its best to spoil Madani's image but masses do not believe it.

The police used *lathis* and broke up the meeting at Calicut and all leaders including Madani were arrested. I was the only person spared. The PDP inauguration was not allowed. The brahminical forces used the Muslim League leaders to attack Madani. See the power of Brahminism.

Today, not only the Muslim League in Kerala but the entire Muslim leadership in the country has been corrupted.

Babri Masjid

That is why even after six months of the Babri Masjid demolition, the Muslim leadership is sleeping on its decision to rebuild the mosque.

Every caste and community leadership has been corrupted. Even the Dalit leadership is corrupted. Corruption is the best and the most effective weapon by which Brahminism kills a community, destroys its identity and then swallows it. Once a community becomes rootless, it decays and falls.

Sikhs, Christians, Tamils have been all swallowed by Brahminism. Enslaved. Brahminism is growing taller, fatter and heavier. Apart from the 15 % Hindus, it derives support from at least 5 to 10% of non-Hindu corrupt followers.

Terrorism in Kashmir

Kashmiris refused to be corrupted and enslaved and that is why they are being violently tackled today through military operation — just like the "Blue Star Operation" (1984) against Sikhs.

Anybody not obeying is called a terrorist, secessionist, separatist, anti-national. Call the dog mad and shoot. This is what is happening in Kashmir today.

Sikhs have been already finished, enslaved by using Sikhs only. Jat Sikhs (K.P.S. Gill) were used to kill Jat Sikhs.

Advocates of BSO say that Brahminism is the world's best religion and a sure solution to all human problems. If this is true, why Brahminism has not been able to solve Brahmins' own poverty? Brahmins very often complain that there are good lot of "poor" Brahmins among them. They demand job reservations on par with SC/STs. What does it prove?

If the *Vedas, Upanishads* and all their Sacred Scriptures are the panacea for all the ills of our society, why these scriptures have not cured the Brahmins' own illness?

The advocates of the BSO are also our rulers. They occupy all important positions from President and Prime Minister of India down to bank managers. Every sector of our society is headed by a Brahmin or a member of the BSO.

Siege mentality

And they defend their monopoly saying that upper castes alone have the "merit and efficiency". If so, why the country is at the bottom of the world? Why India is being pushed out from the Third World to the Fourth World? Why these merit-mongers have failed to give proof of their "merit"?

I will have to conclude. If the country is what it is today, the sole responsibility rests on Brahminism.

This all-round moral corruption, decay, utter chaos and confusion, total breakdown of law and order, environmental crisis and the rising violence are all due to one sole single factor - Brahminism.

The BSO owns a majority of the country's properties, all important positions, wields all the power. BSO is the master of everything. And yet why it is suffering from a siege mentality? This is because the members of this Brahminical Social Order suffer from a peculiar mental disease that has turned them into kill-joys. They think they can be happy only if others are miserable.

This is something unheard of in the whole world. Is it possible to create a tiny island of happiness with filth and misery surrounding all over? Such a thinking defies history.

But the BSO is an exception to this universal rule. BSO thinks it can be happy only at the cost of others' happiness.

Extra peg

If the Muslims are crushed and killed the BSO gets a vicarious pleasure. On the day Babri Masjid was demolished members of the BSO jumped with joy and downed an extra peg.

(laughter). The same BSO derived supreme satisfaction when thousands of Sikhs were killed in the "Blue Star Operation". It gives them immense joy when SC/STs are denied reservations. The BSO thinks it can benefit by denying the reservations to Backward Castes as recommended by the Mandal Commission. Other's suffering brings joy to BSO. Other's pain brings it pleasure. Have you heard of a people like this anywhere in the world?

Battlefield

That is why I have called this a mental disease. BSO's mental disease has converted India into a huge mental hospital.

It needs a psychiatrist. The victims of Brahminism are not only those outside the BSO but members of the BSO themselves — particularly the Brahmin women. It is our duty to cure its mental disorder and bring it back to sanity to restore the country to its original splendour and assure the human rights of the members of BSO itself and thereby liberate ourselves and the country.

That is all I have to say. The 20th century is coming to an end and with it the "Gandhian Era" is also coming to an end. The 21st century will be Dr. Babasaheb Ambedkar's and Sri Narayana Guru's Era. We have to get ready. (*cheers*).

IX - Saffronisation — What it Means to Dalits & Religious Minorities

Lecture delivered to Christian priests, nuns & lay persons on "Target of saffronisation: Religious minorities or who else?" at the Indian Social Institute, Bangalore on March 7, 2002.

We are in the midst of a very tension-packed period because for the first time every section of the country's population is one way or other affected by the violent churning that is going on in the society. If it had not been so, church leaders like you would never have come to this workshop in such big numbers - that too senior level people. That proves even the church is affected by the current churning process. India's Christian population is too small. Not even 3% of the country's population. Though your influence is far greater.

Show other cheek

India's Christian policy, which comes out of your Christian value system, is to remain neutral. Jesus Christ is said to have asked his Christian followers that if somebody slaps on one cheek, they should show the other cheek. Even during the worst attack on church leaders and properties, even when priests and nuns were killed, there was hardly any reaction from Christians. However, it should be remembered that only Dalit Christians and their churches have been attacked by the Hindu nazis. Upper caste Christians have not been the target of nazis. You know the reason? Upper caste Christians and the upper caste Hindu nazis are cousins. But even this passive, peace-loving Christians have been whipped up from their deep slumber and thrown into the boiling cauldron. This is a welcome development.

Hiding enemy's identity

The organisers of this meeting have described this churning process as "saffronisation". I don't agree with this name "saffronisation". The correct name is *brahminisation*. If you say "saffronisation", you are really hiding the identity of the Enemy.

You will be able to correctly understand and appreciate the truth of this statement and the significance of *brahminisation* if I place before you the population breakup of this country.

Unless you know the population breakup, you will not be able to understand not only what is going on in the "saffronisation" front, the latest being the horrendous Gujarat anti-Muslim riots (2002) — the worst carnage after the 1947 partition of India.

Secrecy on population figures

This population figure is kept a top-secret. Newspapers will not publish it. Even some teachers like you are not allowed to know these figures. In this country, Truth is never revealed. Truth is never published because Truth hurts. And our upper castes, who have now become the rulers of India, hate Truth. There are any number of sections in the Indian Penal Code (IPC) to see that the Truth never comes out. I am saying this as a victim of this IPC several times.

Those interested in "saffronising" India, sorry *brahminising* India, will not allow you to know the Truth about India's population breakup. What is this breakup?

I	II
Muslims 15%	Scheduled Castes 20%
Christians 2.5%	Scheduled Tribes .. 10%
Sikhs 2.5%	Backward Castes . 35%
20 +	65% Total: 85%.

Muslims, Christians and Sikhs are called "minorities'. This itself is a wrong name.

Because these "minorities" are the real majority in India.The three "minorities" are definitely not Hindu. There is no confusion or difference of opinion on this point.

The second one lists SC/ST/BCs. Together the three sections make up a staggering 65% of the Indian population.

War on Mandal Commission Report

Are the SC/ST/BCs facing any trouble from the Muslims, Christians or Sikhs? Who is coming in the way of the SC/ST reservation? Is it Muslim, Christian or Sikh?

Who launched the war and violence against the Mandal Commission Report in 1991? Who is preventing Dalits from entering temples?

The unanimous answer to all these questions is upper castes. The other name for these upper castes is Hindu.

If the SC/ST/BCs are also Hindu why the Hindus are coming in the way of their human rights?

So, it must be clear by now that SC/ST/BCs are not Hindu. If both the sections are Hindus and brothers, why the upper castes hate the SC/ST/BCs? So it is clear that the upper castes/ Hindus kick, kill, burn, rape and destroy the little property of SC/ST/BCs because they are not Hindu.

Dr. Ambedkar's verdict

Dr. Ambedkar was the first man to say this. He said the Untouchables are not Hindu but a separate element. Tribals anyway do not live with Hindus.

The first section (Muslim/Christian/Sikh) constitutes 20%. This any way is not Hindu. The second section SC/ST/BCs are also not Hindu.

This section is 65% And 65 + 20 = 85%. That means 85% of India's population is not Hindu. This is the population breakup of India.

But what do the newspapers, our textbooks, our government and all our learned elders say? They say over 85% of Indians are Hindu.

But facts given by me have proved that over 85% of the

population is not Hindu. I have repeated these figures in all my writings and speeches. At one meeting, a top Brahmin social scientist of India, Dr. M.N. Srinivas, was presiding. He never contradicted it. How can he challenge facts of history? Hence he preferred to be silent.

Micro-minority ruling India

The Hindus are only 15% of the population.

But we the over 85% of the *Bahujans*, oppressed by the Brahmins, have no media or propaganda machinery to make this fact known to our own people. That is how facts have become fiction and vice-versa. This is our greatest tragedy.

And even in this 15%, the leaders of thought and action are only Brahmins who are not even 5%. May be about 3%. This 3% micro-minority is ruling India. How can a mere 3% of the people rule over 97% of the population? Is this possible? Is there any such example anywhere else in the world?

The secret of "saffronisation" or to be precise *brahminisation* is the rule of this micro-minority of *vaidiks*.

The 15% Hindus are qlso not a united house. The break-up of this 15% is like this:

Brahmins	3%
Kshatriyas	1%
Vaishya	1%
Shudras	10%
Total=	**15%**

Brahmin killed Gandhi

The Brahmins hate the Vaishyas. That is why a Brahmin killed the Gujarati Bania (Vaishya), M.K. Gandhi. (V.T. Rajshekar: *Why Godse Killed Gandhi*? DSA-1998).

The Brahmins also hate the Kshatriyas. That is why V.P. Singh was quickly removed as Prime Minister. A dwarf Brahmin called

Parasuram went round the "earth" several times and killed all the Kshatriyas. So goes the story in the brahminical literature.

H.D. Deve Gowda, a *shudra* Prime Minister, was given not even six months. Lal Bahadur Shastri, also a *shudra,* was killed within two years.

How then this less than 3% of Brahmins are able to rule us from 1947 with every Prime Minister being a Brahmin (with some minor exceptions)?

The Brahmins who are just 3% of India know their terrible numerical weakness. They are deeply worried that in these days of caste-based electoral politics, they have no future because their *jati* has no strength of numbers.

Weakness of grass-eaters

Apart from being grass-eaters, they are also physically weak fellows.

That is why they have evolved some ingenious strategies and tactics, one of which is saffronisation or *hinduisation* (or *brahminisation*).

I recommend a wonderful book on this subject by Christophe Jeffrelot, a French scholar. He gives full details of the Brahmin efforts to *hinduise* India. (*The Hindu Nationalist Movement & Indian Politics,* 1999 pp.600, Penguin India).

Among the many strategies and tactics evolved by Brahmins, the most important is *hinduisation* (enslavement) of non-Hindu of SC/ST/BCs. By this *hinduisation,* this micro-minority of Brahmins are able to kill two birds (sometimes three birds) with one stone.

After destroying the most popular Budhism, which swept the whole country and driving it out of India, the Brahmins manufactured two epics — *Ramayana* and *Mahabharata* — and then resorted to a wholesale cultural aggression on the indigenous SC/ST/BCs, whom they hate, and thereby they tried to *hinduise* them. (V.T. Rajshekar: *Aggression on Indian Culture,*

DSA - 2001). The non-Hindu SC/ST/BCs, who form 65% of the population, are made to forget their rich history, their traditions, deities, their customs and manners, their food habits, even parents.

In one word their **identities** are being gradually destroyed. (V.T. Rajshekar: *Grave-Diggers of History*, DSA-2001).

In its place, the Brahmins supplied them two brahminical gods —but non-Brahmins —Rama and Krishna, and their Hindu religion.

Cultural Aggression

This process of *hinduisation* of the non-Hindu SC/ST/BCs went on for several centuries but after "independence", (1947) when the Brahmins took direct control of India, the *hinduisation* process gained greater speed. The Rashtriya Swayamsevak Sangh (RSS), the topmost terrorist organisation of "Sacred Brahmins", has established numerous well-funded fronts to undertake this job. The brahminical monopoly media is working overtime to speed up the *hinduisation* (enslavement) of the non-Hindu SC/ST/BCs. And I can say with authority that the Hindu nazis are doing a commendable job and they have almost succeeded in converting the non-Hindu India into their *Hindu Rashtra* dreamland. That is how the three non-Hindu sections, who are not Hindus, are made Hindus.

What do the Brahmins gain out of *hinduising* the non-Hindus? The gain is tremendous. The mere 15% Hindus suddenly become 85%, their religion of Hinduism becomes the "majority religion". And more than anything else, the Brahmin who stands at the apex of the caste pyramid, becomes the automatic leader of the Hindu society.

After having become the leader of the entire Hindu society and having converted India into a *Hindu Rashtra*, his next target is to inject the Hindu hatred into innocent SC/ST/BCs and instigate them against Muslim/Christian/Sikh. The Brahmins finished the Sikhs in 1984 itself ("Blue Star Operation"). About 3,500 Sikhs — men, women and children — were killed in the Sikhs' holiest Golden Temple and the great Sikh saint, Sant Bhindranwale, who can be ranked next only to Guru Gobind Singh, was killed in the army operation. This was the last resistance offered by the Sikhs whose very revolutionary religion was born to liberate the oppressed Dalits from the clutches of upper castes. After this the upper caste Sikhs simply surrendered to the Hindus and became their bodyguards even to the extent of becoming anti-Muslim (Dr. K.K. Sidhu: *How Vaidiks Turned Sikhs into Muslim-Haters*, DSA-2002). Sikhism has been totally *hinduised* (enslaved). We have almost lost hope in Sikhism. A great religion has been simply killed.

Non-violence as a weapon

The beauty of Brahminism is that it seldom employs violent means to finish the adversary. The use of the Indian Army to destroy the Sikh backbone was an exception. *Vaidiks* are experts in using cultural aggression to dilute and destroy its adversaries. The most effective cultural aggression that finished the Sikhs was the *vaidik* invention of Arya Samaj.

Christians are being targeted now. The killing of the Australian missionary, Stains, was the beginning of this anti-Christian war and violence.

When the Sikhs were subjected to mass murder in 1984, the Christians did not get angry. Nor did they wake up to the danger posed by these Hindu nazis when the Babri Masjid was demolished in 1992. The Christians woke up only now.

But the Christians are the country's most educated and also conscious people. If such a brilliant people with a country-wide network are not able to understand the danger posed by Brahmins, you can imagine the plight of unlettered, poverty-stricken, unconscious SC/ST/BCs.

The Gujarat genocide of Muslims (2002) is a proof of the

efficacy of the "saffronisation" or *hinduisation* of India. Not a single Brahmin, Bania or Patel died in the three-day peak violence that shook Gujarat in Feb.-March 2002. Those who died were mostly Muslims and some SC/ST/BCs.

The upper castes have succeeded in painting the Muslims in black and portraying them as terrorists, criminals, anti-nationals, anti-woman, dirty, smugglers. All types of adjectives are applied against this community that ruled this country for 800 years. Within 60 years, such a great community that contributed so much for the cultural enrichment of India and liberation of its oppressed people, victims of Brahminism, has been enslaved. No doubt, in the case of Muslims there is no hesitation to employ violence. Since the state itself has become Hindu in India, state terrorism against Muslims is not considered wrong by anybody.

Serpent & mongoose

In the Gujarat genocide, the Gujarati Bania Chief Minister, Narendra Modi, himself encouraged the Muslim mayhem.

The beauty is that the upper castes do not come and kill Muslims. This job of killing Muslims is done by the non-Hindu SC/ST/BCs after they have been **made** Hindu. And every Hindu is a born enemy of the Muslim. This is the result of the Hindu nazi "cultural revolution" which is at full play since they demolished the Muslim Babri Masjid (1992).

The Muslims are being killed in large numbers because they are considered enemies of Hinduism. Islam and Hinduism are like serpent and mongoose. The value system of Islam is juxtaposed to Hinduism (M.N. Ray: *Historical Role of Islam*, Ajanta Publications, Delhi, 1981). Revolutionary Islam has all the ability to destroy the religion of upper castes. Nobody knows it better than the *vaidiks*. Having identified their enemy, the *vaidiks* are now using the non-Hindu Dalits and SC/ST/BCs to destroy Islam.

Look at the *vaidik* strategy. They used their non-Hindu enemies, SC/ST/BCs, to kill the Muslims and in the process SC/ST/BCs were also killed by Muslims. In the Godhra railway station incident, which sparked off the Gujarat Muslim genocide, all those who died were the SC/ST/BC *Ram sevaks*, used as slaves of Hindus.

See how beautifully and effectively they divided the society and enforced their rule. No Brahmin, Bania or Patel died. Chief Minister Narendra Modi and his fellow Hindus all over India did not shed even a drop of tear over the Gujarat violence.

No Shankarachari raised any religious objection to the killings. All of them were happy. And yet these Hindus say that theirs is the world's only religion that preaches non-violence.

Religion of hate

This is Hinduism, a religion of hate which is the staple diet of Hindus.

The second part of the subject given for my talk speaks about the "implication of saffronisation on minority rights". Actually, this part is more important.

The Hindus (upper castes) make it appear that they and their party, BJP - *Brahmana Jati Party* — is for Hindus and hence opposed to Muslims and Christians, who are dubbed anti-Hindus. This is a wrong interpretation of the Hindu nazi party ideology.

Christians educating only Hindus

The Brahmins and their 15% Hindus were never against "religious minorities". Certainly not against Christians. Nor are they against Muslims and Christians today.

Go to any elite Christian educational institution in India, specially convents. Who are the students making full use of these schools and colleges? Mostly Brahmins and other upper castes.

Students belonging to SC/ST/BCs do not get admission to these institutions. The Christian management of these institutions itself is against Dalits. Even their own co-religionist Dalit Christian students do not get admission to these institutions. (V.T. Rajshekar: *Christians & Dalit Liberation*, DSA-2000).

During the British (Christian) rule the Brahmins held top positions. They were the first to get English education and because of this they were the first to get jobs under the British Government.

Not only that. The Brahmins were also the first to get converted to Christianity. De Nobili, a Western missionary who did most of the early conversions in Western India, preferred the Brahmins to expand the Christian population.

Then how do you say that the Hindus are against Christians?

Muslims helped Brahmins

During the 800 years of Muslim rule, Brahmins were holding top positions. Their girls married Muslim rulers. Brahmins were Dewans and advisers. Both the White Western Christians and Muslims who came to India were fair-skinned and preferred the fair-skinned Brahmins and other upper castes.

So it is wrong to say that Hindus (upper castes) are against Christians and Muslims. May be to some extent Muslims, but certainly they do not hate Christians.

Havoc played by Ganapati

The Hindu hate campaign against Muslims is also a recent development. May be about 150 years. It was Bal Gangadhar Tilak, a Chitpavan Brahmin from Pune, who engineered the first anti-Muslim riot in Bombay by inventing a new god called Ganapati who today has overtaken all other gods and has become the No.1 among the 330 million Hindu gods.

What Hindus hate is conversion

As for the Sikhs, they have been swallowed long back and in 1984 (Blue Star Operation) the Sikh back was completely broken.

Brahmins and their Hindus do not hate Christians. What they hate is Christian conversion of SC/ST/BCs. Because conversion reduces the number of Hindus.

Already in Kerala, the Christian population has gone up to 25%. In Andhra Pradesh and Tamil Nadu also it is going up. The Hindu rulers oppose Dalit Christian demand for reservation only because of this reason. Once this ban on reservation is removed there will be an exodus of Dalits to Christianity. Though the Constitution as such has no bar on conversion, the Hindu rulers have passed some legislations that come in the way of conversions. The courts in India, including the Supreme Court being upper caste-dominated, uphold these legislations despite being unconstitutional. Hindus have no respect for the Constitution of India. Anything that goes against their *dharma* (meaning Brahminism) is struck down by the court itself.

Cousins & blood brothers

The Hindu rulers of India are very much worried about conversions though conversions have very much helped the Untouchables in securing religious and social liberation. (Dr. B.R. Ambedkar: *Why Go for Conversion?*, DSA-1983). Hinduism is not bothered about what happens to Dalits as long as it does not reduce the number of Dalits within the Hindu fold.

So, it must be clear now that Hindus do not hate the Christians and their church as long as they do not resort to religious conversions.

The upper caste Christians like the Syrians, Goans and Mangalorean Christians, who have captured the church leadership, agree with the Hindu argument because both are cousins and blood brothers. The church is happy with the Hindus and Hindus are happy with the church. The White Western Christians countries which finance the Indian Christians are also happy. Then who said the Hindus hate Christians? It is all bullshit.

Rather, the Hindus love the Christians because church is beautifully serving the Hindus.

It is racial hatred

Why the Hindus (upper castes) are against non-Hindu SC/ST/ BCs? Because the Hindus are Aryans and fair-skinned, and the non-Hindus are the children of this soil and dark-skinned.

The Hindu hostility against the indigenous Indians is a racial hatred.

This hatred is as old as about 3,000 to 4,000 years. The Durban Conference (2001) of the United Nations has proved this point. (DV Edit Oct.1, 2001: "*World comes to know of racism in Hindu India: Gang of Three stand isolated at Durban conference*").

India's greatest and the most liberating religion of Budhism was destroyed and driven out of India because of this Aryan hatred of the indigenous peoples.

Both the *Ramayana* and the *Mahabharata* speak of the defeat of the indigenous peoples of India.

The three "minority" religions of India — Islam, Christianity and Sikhism — became popular because they were liberating religions and fought the Aryan brahminical imperialism.

Indian history itself is a series of clash between Aryans and non-Aryans.

The upper castes (Hindus) are not so much worried about the three religious minorities. They have finished all of them. Even the revolutionary Islam has been made to bend and beg before the Brahmin. (V.T. Rajshekar: *How to Exterminate Muslims in India?*, DSA - 2001).

Brahmins never suffered defeat

They might have failed once in 1992. But you can take it from me, they **will** build their Ram temple on the demolished Babri Masjid site.

Remember, the triumphant Brahminism never suffered even a minor setback, never a defeat, even once. Their biggest obstacle was Budhism. Once they destroyed and drove it out of India, they never faced any road-block. There were innumerable anti-Brahmin movements led by Guru Nanak, Mahatma Phule, Basaveshwara, Sri Naryana Guru, Periyar E.V. Ramaswamy, Dr. Ambedkar. But the Brahmins successfully destroyed each of them by using the caste contradictions in the Indian society. Now that they have become the rulers with the government in their hand, and more than that the entire media becoming a Brahmin monopoly, I don't know how it is possible to dislodge them.

There has been such a fierce attack on the church in India. Did any White Western Christian country on whose money India, a beggar nation, is surviving, cut its aid? Did the World Bank punish India? Did the Pope get angry? Did the World Council of Churches pass any strictures against their White Western governments financially supporting India? Never.

The White Western countries are racists and India's Aryan brahminical forces are the founding fathers of racism. The two have now come together.

That is why the Western Christian countries are not listening to the cries of Indian Christians.

It was our friend, John Dayal, a dark-looking Roman Catholic of Delhi, who rattled the church and raised the Hindu persecution of Indian church to international heights. But his is a lone cry. But I don't think the White Western Christian leadership heart is melting. India's church leadership supported the Indian Dalit demand that "casteism is racism" at the UN World Conference Against Racism at Durban (2001) but at this very same conference the White Western racists, supported by the American Christian rulers, opposed the Afro-American (Blacks) demand for reparations. The World Council of

Churches and the Roman Catholic church should have supported the Black demand and also the demand of India's Black Untouchables. But they did not. Does it not prove that the Western church leadership will not support the campaigns of John Dayal and his Dalit Christians friends in India? Except lip sympathy he will not get anything.

Hence the urgent need for Dalit Christians to join hands with India's Dalits — The Black Untouchables.

The brahminical rulers have come to know that the church in India is not only weak but badly divided. They also know that the upper caste church leaders are persecuting their own Dalit Christians.

In other words the brahminical forces are not targeting Muslims and Christians.

The real enemy of the Hindu is the non-Hindu SC/ST/BCs, mainly the Dalits who are the blood enemies of Brahmins.

Identify the Enemy

The church says it is doing so much for the Dalits and Tribals.

If this is true, it must place all its resources, manpower and institutions at the disposal of Dalits, make them aware of the Enemy and support Dalit struggle against Brahminism.

Nobody in India has fought the Brahmins so effectively and so scientifically as Dr. Babasaheb.

Please make a study of Dr. Ambedkar's thoughts and help Dalits to carry out the mission of Babasaheb.

Aim of *hinduisation*

Hinduisation or saffronisation, therefore, means keeping the people enslaved under the brahminical leadership. This brahminical leadership talks as if it is a great votary of democracy. But is the Brahminical Social Order (BSO) democratic?

Leadership of any society or country has to be chosen by the people and elected under a democratic process. But in India, the BSO cannot get elected because it has no numerical strength. Brahmins as such are only about 3% and barring the *shudras*, the other two — the Kshatriyas and Vaishyas — are less than 1%.

The status of *shudras*

The *shudras* hate the Brahmins. Every anti-Brahmin movement in India was led by the *shudras* once upon a time. The very word *shudra* in Sanskrit means children born to the SC/ST/BC non-Hindu concubines of Brahmins. In other words, *shudra* means bastards. *Shudras* are held in extreme contempt in the BSO. The SC/ST/BC being the original inhabitants of India know their fathers and mothers. They are not bastards but the *shudras* are neither with the SC/ST/BCs nor with the twice-born (*dwija*). Rather they are hated by both. Such is their pitiable condition. Yet the *shudras* prefer to go with the BSO despite all the degrading status assigned to it.

The Jats of Hindi belt and the Sikh Jats of Punjab are the best example to prove how the *shudras* continue to lick the shoes of the Brahmins despite all the ill-treatment meted out to them by the BSO.

The *shudras*, who rank fourth and the last in the Hindu (BSO) hierarchy, are mostly land-owners and physically strong. The Brahmins while keeping them at a distance made full use of the *shudras* to keep a check on the non-Hindu SC/ST/BCs who are outside the four-fold caste system (BSO). Taking advantage of the caste contradictions between the *shudras* and the SC/BCs, the Brahmins with the help of their media made the latter turn against them.

Death of Periyar movement

The best example is Tamil Nadu (TN). The *shudras* were in the forefront of the anti-Brahmin movement in TN. All the top leaders of the Periyar E.V. Ramaswamy movement were *shudras*. C.N. Annadurai was a Mudaliar (*shudra*) who became the first Chief Minister of TN, forming a political party out of the Periyar movement. All *shudras* joined the movement. As the class-caste interests of the *shudras* were antagonistic to that of the BCs and SCs, the two got divided and the Brahmins fanning the flames of hatred between the two got them separated from each other. Today the Periyar movement is virtually dead.

The *shudras*, who ousted the Brahmins in TN, occupied their seats as rulers and started persecuting the SC/ST/BCs and Muslims of TN (*Rise, fall and slow death of Periyar movement in TN*", reprint of *Caravan* article, 1979).

Similarly in the neighbouring Kerala, the *shudra* Nairs were the leaders of the anti-Brahmin movement but today the brahminical Hindu nazi movement is led by the *shudra* Nairs.

Fall of *Shudra* Marathas

In Maharashtra, the *Shudra* Marathas have been the worst enemies of Brahmins.

Shivaji, the most famous Maratha leader, was the victim of Brahmin machinations. But today the same Marathas have become the most loyal servants of Brahmins who brought about a cleavage between the Marathas and the Dalits. The land-owning Marathas preferred to go with the Brahmins and got themselves totally alienated from the rest of the Maharashtrians.

The same thing is true in rest of India also.

Identity destroyed

The *vaidiks* destroyed the social harmony in India. One *jati* has come to hate the other. During elections the caste (*jati*) comes to the fore because electoral politics needs strength of numbers which can come only from one's caste. Elections in

India are virtually turning into a trial of strength between one *jati* and the other. Caste rivalry has become extremely serious and this is one of the disastrous results of the *hinduisation* for which nobody else can be blamed except the Brahmins.

The different *jatis* coming under the SCs and BCs are gradually losing their **identity** under this rapid *hinduisation* process. Each *jati* had its own distinct **identity** — its own customs, manners, deities, festivals, food habits, dress, historical traditions. But under the impact of *hinduisation*, these *jatis* are fast losing their **identity**. Losing **identity** is like the fall of a tree when its roots are cut or decayed. When the roots die, the tree falls. Each *jati* in India had its own strong roots in history. The very object of *hinduisation* is to destroy the roots of a *jati* and thereby felling the tree.

Backward Caste movement killed

The worst impact of this can be found on the Backward Castes who form a formidable 35% of the country's population. The country once had a strong BC movement. Dr. Ambedkar's Dalit movement was born as a result of the BC movement led by Mahatma Jyotirao Phule. But the Hindu nazis with their hyper activities of *hinduisation* have killed the BC movement. The Mandal Commission report that conferred reservations (human rights) on BCs is forgotten by the BCs themselves because the BCs are today in the forefront of the Hindu nazi movement. *Hinduisation* destroyed the BC movement that had a great historical past. Today, no part of India has any BC movement worth the name. Not even South India which once had a strong BC movement. The BCs are busy carrying the shoes of the Brahmins. Where is the time (forget about the brain) for them to think of the BC movement? Look, how history has been reversed and a great cluster of communities numbering 35% of the country's population, which once produced Dr. Ram Manohar Lohia, was simply killed. The Hindu nazis in their *hinduisation* process have destroyed the human rights of 35% of India's population.

Having succeeded with the BCs, the nazis are now trying to bulldoze and destroy the Dalit movement. The entire leadership of Dalits and Tribals has been corrupted and co-opted. The educated and employed Dalits and Tribals have forgotten their roots, married upper caste girls and taken to Hindu way of life. Even the Dr. Ambedkar movement is in the process of dying. *Hinduisation* of Tribals is in full swing and the very first Tribal state (Jharkhand) formed in India is under the Hindu nazi party.

Painful process

So you can imagine the serious impact of *hinduisation* on the social fabric of India. SC/ST/BCs are fast being made slaves. *Hinduisation* of the non-Hindu SC/ST/BCs is, therefore, a painful process. Over 65% of the population is in a state of ferment. As they fast lose their **identity** they also lose their status in society and become no people. They become a sort of fish out of water. Loss of **identity** is accompanied by their pauperisation. SC/ST/BCs are reduced to lumpen proletariat. and when such a huge population sinks, the country also sinks along with them. In other words, *hinduisation* leads to degeneration and gradual decay of India. But the *vaidiks* are unperturbed.

Muslims and Christians, therefore, are not the enemies of the Hindu nazi party. *Hinduisation* process does not target them. They are using the Muslims and Christians as the whipping boys. Their real target is the SC/ST/BCs and to finish them, the Hindu nazis have manufactured two enemies — Muslims and Christians. And they point out these two "minorities" as the enemies of India so that the SC/ST/BCs are kept busy attacking and killing the two enemies.

Such a frequent fight between the two oppressed, poverty-stricken communities will keep the two sections busy and also away from the real enemy which is sucking the blood of both

SC/ST/BCs and the Muslim/Christian/Sikhs. Can you think of a better or a more brilliant strategy and tactic to enslave the world's second largest populated country?

India fast going down hill

H*indulsation,* therefore, is a very painful process. A huge mass of over 85% of the population is all the time kept busy sniping at each other, killing each other and destroying each other's property.

Nowhere and at no time in Indian history, Muslims, Christians or Sikhs have persecuted the SC/ST/BCs nor vice-versa.

The three "minority" religions were born to liberate these very three sections. Today, the Brahmins have so cunningly turned these very three sections against Muslims, Christians and Sikhs.

Since the entire intellectual class in India happens to be the upper caste, there is none in India to write on such a subject. And if anybody outside the BSO takes up such a mission, the very hounds of the *hinduised* state machinery are there to pounce upon such a writer.

Both the Muslims/Christians and SC/ST/BCs are the victims of the same BSO. It is a historical fact that the *hinduisation* process has diverted the attention of both the sections from the real enemy to an imaginary enemy. And in the process one brother is made to fight and kill the other brother.

How can at this rate of a daily war and violence all over India, the people can think of reconstructing and rebuilding the society? Their entire time, energy and little money is spent only on daily war and violence.

Muslims who ruled India for 800 years have been enslaved, pauperised and more than anything dubbed terrorist, anti-nationals and being shot dead.

The entire social fabric of India is torn to pieces. And such criminals who brought about such a disruption of social, economic, cultural and political life of India describe themselves as "nationalists" while in fact there can be no greater anti-nationals than the Hindu nazis.

The country has been fast slipping downwards. We can get all the statistics from the official records itself. While every country that became independent after India has galloped and marched forward, we have been busy quarreling between ourselves. Like those crabs kept in a basket. We don't allow the others to go up.

Indians need have no enemies because we are our own enemies under the existing Hindu nazi rule.

But the BSO is not worried over the country going downhill as a result of this painful *hinduisation* drive. As long as the Brahmin is allowed to remain as the supreme leader, he does not care what happens to the country. He does not care for the country because as Aryans and foreigners to India, this country does not belong to him. The sole interest of the Brahmin is to rule India at any cost.

Hinduisation has sapped the energies of the people and made them lifeless.

Why West is silent

But the White Western racists, who are the first to flaunt the human rights records of a country, are silent about India - the graveyard of human rights. This is because those who rule India are the blood brothers of the White Western racist rulers. Both are Aryans. Hence this silence on the part of West on the crimes committed by the Hindu rulers of India.

ANNEXURE -1

Jewish Scholar who Diagnosed Disease of Brahminism but Failed to Cure it

With deep sorrow we announce the death of a distinguished French historian, Leon Poliakov, whose book, *The Aryan Myth* (1977, New American Library, New York), had stunned us by its shocking revelations of the havoc played by Brahminism and made us realise that Brahminism was a threat not only to India but to the whole world causing two World Wars and now conspiring a more deadly Third World War.

In this book, the author, also a distinguished member of the *Dalit Voice* family world-wide in the early 80s, says the "Aryan Myth" was created by the German Christians to fight the Roman Catholic church which had turned oppressive. The book reveals that the Aryan Brahmins of India fooled even the Germans, considered to be the world's most brilliant people.

Jews as victims of Brahminism

For the first time in the history of the world, the "Aryan Myth" manufactured by the cunning brahminical races caused an avalanche of hatred against women, Blacks, Muslims, India's Untouchables and, according to Poliakov, caused even an anti-Jew war and violence.

This is what made us to describe Brahminism as the "Father of Fascism"

Leon Poliakov (87) was himself a Jew and we bow our head before his scholarship. It was from his book that we learnt that even Jews were victims of Brahminism which brainwashed the Germans and Adolf Hitler to declare Jews as enemies being non-Aryan and killed millions of Jews in gas chamber.

He found fault with our thesis that the *Vaidik* Brahmins and

Jews had the same qualities and took objection to our description that the Brahmins indeed are the "Jews of India".

A Paris datelined AP report published in the *Times of India*, Bangalore (Dec.11, 1997), said:

> Leon Poliakov, a Russian-born writer who fought for the French resistance and became one of the world's most respected historians of anti-Semitism, has died, Jewish organisations said on Dec.9. He was 87.
>
> In a statement, the Representative Council of Jewish Organisations, called Poliakov a pioneer who turned the study of anti-Semitism into "a scientific discipline in its own right".
>
> Poliakov demonstrated that "the extermination of Jews by the Nazis was the culmination of a long history of humiliation and oppression".
>
> He was best-known for his four-volume *History of Anti-Semitism* published between 1956 and 1977, which examined the Christian roots of anti-Jewish sentiment. A fifth volume of essays on anti-Semitism in post-War France appeared in 1994.

Mrs. Yumi Tsuji, a noted Japanese scholar and student of Leon Poliakov at Paris, who presented us the *Aryan Myth* book at Tokyo on Sept.13, 1982, also sought apology from us for describing the Brahmins as the "Jews of India". We did tender the apology in our earlier version of the book, but in the second enlarged edition of the book, *Brahminism - Father of Fascism* (1994), we added a chapter titled: "Poliakov proved wrong on Jews of India".

4,000-year-old war

If the alien Aryan *Vaidik* Brahmin races were responsible for selling their "Aryan Myth" to Germans and thereby brainwashing them to kill Jews in millions, as Poliakov argues in his book, the Jews should have been the greatest friends of India's Black Untouchables who are the worst victims of Brahminism. In fact, the Untouchables (Dalits), the original inhabitants of India, have been fighting the invading Aryan races from the very beginning. The history of their anti-Aryan war is as old as 4,000 years. But to our utter shock not only the Jews have joined hands with the "Jews of India" but together they are today trying to destroy India's unity and integrity.

While the Dalits never compromised with the Aryans, how did the Jews compromise and collaborate with the "Jews of India?"

We pointed out this fact to Poliakov but he maintained silence.

What brought the Jews and the "Jews of India" together is perhaps their common hatred of Muslims. And India has the world's largest Muslim population after Indonesia.

Spanish experiment

Poliakov nowhere in his book refers to any hatred between the Jews and Muslims. In fact, he is critical of the "Spanish Experiment" which annihilated Islam in Spain and made it a Christian country (DV Editorial May 16, 1985: "*How to exterminate Muslims in India - Hindu nazis following Spanish experiment*").

Poliakov was right in saying that it was the Brahmins who supplied the swastika symbol to Hitler, described the Germans as Aryans and thereby inspired the growth of nazism that caused the terrible anti-Jew pogrom. This fact may not be known to the ordinary Jew but the Jewish leadership and particularly the zionist brains know it.

The *Aryan Myth* book itself was the product of a research foundation set up by the Jews. And that means the Jewish Diaspora think-tank is aware of the havoc caused by the "Aryan Myth" propounded by Brahmins and how millions of Jews were allegedly exterminated by this Aryan philosophy of hate.

Zionist control of world

Zionists today not only control the entire world finance and media but the entire Government of the United States of America. Nothing can happen in the world without the sanction of the zionist leadership. Such is the power of the zionists world-wide.

This writer had written several letters, published many articles and finally wrote a book itself, *Brahminism - Father of Fascism*, and sincerely hoped that the Jews and the zionist leadership would respond. But sorry to note that the venerable author of the *Aryan Myth*, who is no more, and the entire zionist leadership refused to react.

We wrote three letters to the Israeli Embassy in Delhi which refused even to acknowledge our letters.

Germans deceived

But the silence is no reflection on the great work of Leon Poliakov, his sincerity and devotion to his community of Jews who were the bloody victims of Brahminism.

Poliakov's research conclusively proves that it was Brahminism which inspired and instigated the Germans to kill Jews and caused two World Wars. He accuses Nietzsche, Max Muller and a host of indologists who were deceived by the "Aryan Myth" and mis-directed the Germans to annihilate the Jews.

The foundations of the "Aryan Myth" are built on hate, prejudice, narcissism. Dalits, Muslims and the entire indigenous people comprising over 85% of India's population are also the victims of this "Aryan Myth".

If this is so, Poliakov and his zionist think-tank should have teamed up with us.

The Muslims and the Blacks of the world plus India's Black Untouchables are all victims of this Aryan theory of racism, fascism, nazism. Poliakov says all this.

Jews guided by "Jews of India"

If Poliakov and his zionist think tank have traced the origin of racism, fascism and nazism to Brahminism, why they have remained silent on the sufferings of India's Untouchables, and also the persecution of Blacks by Whites and the Muslims world over?

The silence is intriguing. This is where we suspect the sincerity of the zionist think-tank which even forced Poliakov to remain silent on our repeated communications. If they were merely silent or indifferent we could have excused Poliakov and his zionist think-tank. But today the world will be shocked to hear that the Jews are actively guided by the "Jews of India".

Poliakov's book can be described as the world's most authoritative indictment of Brahminism. And yet having diagnosed the disease, Poliakov failed to cure it. He had the intellectual capacity to diagnose the disease but what made him to sulk to take the more important step of curing it? We need the answer.

(Signed article in the *Dalit Voice*, Jan.16, 1998 p. 9-10).

ANNEXURE - 2

Brahminical Origin of Zionist Thoughts

The most important thing we learnt after reading the different documents quoted in the German journal, *Christ State International*, (special edition No.9, May 1992) is the great similarity between the zionist thought and the language used in the Aryan "Sacred Books". Since the Brahminical Social Order is much more ancient it is quite likely that the zionist founding fathers got their inspiration from the BSO.

Dalit Voice has thus proved right in predicting that the Jews and the "Jews of India" will join hands to crush Muslims, Blacks and India's Dalits.

The *Christ State* journal predicts that the zionist "undertaking is doomed to failure..." DV also said the same thing that the Third World War will be engineered by the combined evil forces of nazism, zionism, racism and Brahminism which will meet its defeat in this war.

Control on USA

That means there is a good lot of similarity in the thinking of *Christ State International*, being published from Germany, and *Dalit Voice* from India. Hence the need for close cooperation and collaboration between the two to defend the racially oppressed and enslaved peoples of the world and to ensure world peace and harmony.

The German journal discloses that the American dollar currency note carries the zionist pyramid. Says that of the 56 who signed the American Declaration of Independence in 1776, 50 were Freemasons. The American billionaire, Rockefeller, is repeatedly mentioned as a top zionist functionary. US Presidents, Ronald Reagon, George Bush had close connections. And that is how Bush announced the "New World Order". The new President Clinton is supposed to be a zionist nominee.

It says the United Nations is a slave of the zionists. So also the IMF and the World Bank. More shocking is the disclosure that the Vatican is closely aligned with the zionists. So also the Rotary International and the Lions International.

Mind control

Writing under the headline, "Those controlling the media, also control public opinion,

> it discloses that the zionists have "already succeeded in controlling the thought world... to such an extent that nearly all other citizens who are not insiders look upon the events of the world through the colored glasses which we have put on their noses. (From the *Protocols of the World dictatorship*, Des Griffin: *Who Rules the World*?).

The entire Western world's print and electronic media is under zionist control and how they deliberately put out false reports on the recent Gulf War was reported in *Dalit Voice*.

In another item, "The International secret language of the Freemasons", the journal hints at Gorbachev's zionist connections on the basis of his "forefinger pose". "The raised or outstretched forefinger is the sign language of the zionists".

Theosophy & Brahminism

What will come as a shock to India is the zionist connections of the Theosophical Society and its Russian founder Blavatsky. Theosophy has been the heart of the Tamil Brahmins, many of whom held top positions in the organization. Annie Besant, a British woman who once headed the Congress, India's original brahminical party, was a Theosophist.

The "Bnai Birth" lodge is a secret organization of the zionists claiming leadership over the entire zionist world.

In Germany, the zionists maintain a hold on its government even today.

The journal then profusely quotes from several zionist documents and we have selected some portions to tell our readers how closely it resembles the language used in the "Sacred Texts" of the BSO.

World dictatorship

"The Master Plan for a World Dictatorship" says in 1901 and 1906, an illuminati booklet appeared entitled *Protocols of the Wise Men of Zion*, "which is generally regarded as a more relevant and concrete continuation of the old plan of Weishaupt... (to gain world domination)". Parts of the contents of these protocols are already contained in older documents. In 1919, they appeared for the first time in the German language. We have taken the following excerpts from the "Protocols of the World Dictatorship", as Des Griffin calls the "Protocols of the Wise Men of Zion" in his book *Who Rules the World*:-

Des Griffin bases his statements on a copy of these texts which have been in the British Museum in London since 1906. For obvious reasons, definite proof of the authenticity cannot be given, because clandestine work and secrecy are central factors in the nature of the illuminati. Therefore, no outsider can be sure to what extent the texts are authentic and complete. It is, however, irrefutable that many world events in the last 80 years can be classified under this "General Plan for a World Dictatorship".

True goals disguised: "The external (profane) activities of the Freemasons serve the purpose of disguising our might and its goal: Our war plan, and even the seat of our might, will always remain concealed to the people". (p.264).

Those not obeying will die: "In the Masonic lodges we carry out the death penalty in such a way that no one except for the lodge brothers is able to suspect, not even the victims themselves; they will die, if it is necessary, apparently of a natural death."

"Useful idiots": "We will have mercilessly executed everyone who rebels with arms against us and our authority. Even one setting up any kind of new secret society will likewise be punished with death. We will completely disband all presently existing secret societies which are well known to of all of us and which have served and still do serve us well. Their members shall be sent into exile to continents far removed from Europe".

Power of the press: "We have gained influence through the press, and yet have remained in the shadows. Due to the press, we brought mountains of gold into our hands..." (p.258).

Press censorship: "No single news will reach the public without our control. We have already accomplished this goal, for the most part, in that news items from all parts of the world flow into a few news agencies and only after being edited, are then transmitted to the individual newspaper offices, public authorities and others. These news agencies should gradually come entirely into our possession and publish only that which we dictate." (p.286)

"Furthermore, we are masters in the art of leading the masses and individuals according to our will, by skillful manipulation in the spoken and written word, by elegant manners and by all kinds of tricks about which the non-illumined have no idea". (p. 265)

"News is what we give": "We have already succeeded in controlling the thought world of the non-illumined to such an extent that nearly all other citizens who are not insiders look upon world events through the rose colored glasses which we have set on their noses."

"No media means no voice": "We want to print sometimes the truth, sometimes lie, sometimes facts, sometimes corrections, according to how the public receives the news. It is a part of our principles to cautiously feel the ground before we set foot on it. Because of these methods of dealing with the press, we will surely be victorious over our enemies, since they have no newspapers at their disposal, in which they can fully express their opinion. We will not have to spend any effort in order to refute them." (p. 289)

Tyranny as *Dharma*: "Our kingdom will be characterized by immeasurable tyranny so that it is at all times and everywhere in a position of nipping the resistance of discontented people in the bud". (p.265).

(Signed article in the *Dalit Voice* of Jan.16, 1993).

ANNEXURE - 3

Nazis, Jews & "Jews of India"

Recently, an old member of the *Dalit Voice* family world-wide, Ms. Eva-Maria Hardtman, a distinguished professor in a Swedish University at Stockholm, met us in Delhi and said DV had every potential to emerge as India's foremost human rights journal and scores of Europeans would be too happy to read it.

But, she said, there was a problem with DV. And because of this "problem" the European scholars were hesitating to read DV.

Banned word

What is this "problem"? The "problem" is DV's usage of the words "Hindu nazis" and particularly the "Jews", which, she said, is a racist term and hence banned by the government in Sweden and some other countries.

> "If you want to criticise Jews, don't use that word but say zionist. If you use the word Jews to criticise them you are criticising a particular race which is not allowed. But if you use the word zionist, you will be criticising a philosophy and there will be no objections. In Germany and many other European countries nazism is getting popular. Hitler is gaining followers. So, when you use the words Hindu nazis, admirers of nazism will resent it. For this reason DV is not gaining circulation in Europe".

Sister Eva-Maria is not only our good old family member but a great lover and admirer of DV. She came all the way to Patna some six years ago to be present when we embraced Budhism at a mass conversion ceremony there. Her advice was given in our interest and we really appreciate her sincere concern.

Black Bishop's advice

A similar advice was given to our Black Bishop, Rev. M. Azariah of Madras, when he toured Germany some years back. Germans took strong objection to DV using the word "Hindu nazis". They said many young Germans were becoming nazis and nazism was gaining ground. The use of the word "Hindu nazis" has offended the Germans. The Bishop had to do lot explaining to convince the Germans. But Sister Eva-Maria fully understands and appreciates our dilemma.

When we explained her our difficulties in finding the right words and phrases to describe our upper caste (Aryan) oppressors, whom we call "Hindu nazis", she appreciated our point. She also understood and appreciated our usage of the term "Jews of India" to describe the terrorists among the Indian Aryan *vaidiks.*

Massacre of Jews

If the "Hindu nazis" of India are credited with having inspired Hitler's nazism in Germany and thereby causing the death of millions of Jews, then the same *vaidik* forces in India must be also haters of Jews and zionism. Because the German nazism's sole purpose was to annihilate Jews. If this is the historical truth then naturally India's Hindu nazis like their German counterparts must be anti-Jew. Are they?

The "problem" pointed by Eva-Maria begins here. India's Hindu nazis have no permanent philosophy, no permanent friends or no permanent enemies. They have only permanent interests. As their sole interest is protecting and perpetuating their hate philosophy, which helps keep them as rulers, they change themselves according to the changing times. They change their dress according to the changing weather.

Yesterday, the German nazism helped them to protect and perpetuate themselves. And today, the Jews and their zionism are helping to keep themselves as rulers of India.

This Editorial seeks to elaborate the dilemma facing India's principal oppressed community of Dalits, the Black Untouchables of India. It is a philosophical analysis of the serious dilemma facing us and we hope our family members in Europe and US will understand and appreciate our "problem".

The Untouchables of India form over 20% of India's population and together with Tribals (10%) we become a third of India. Muslims form over 15%. Then comes the Backward Castes (35%) who are also our brothers. So, this Editorial is on the dilemma facing over 85% of India's 1,000 million population, persecuted by the minuscule Hindu nazis who are not even 3% of India's population.

Original home of racism

All philosophers of nazism right from Nietzsche have acknowledged that they were solely inspired by India's Aryan Brahminism and this made us write our first book, *Who is the Mother of Hitler?* (Dalit Sahitya Akademy - 1984).

Every word written in it has proved right: India is the original home of racism and the Aryan *varna* (fair-skinned colour) people are its founding fathers. Here also we proved right. Not only that. We have also proved right in saying that the Aryan *Vaidik* Brahmins of India are also the fathers of zionism.

When Poliakov proved wrong

In our signed article, "*Jewish scholar who diagnosed disease of Brahminism but failed to cure it*", (*Dalit Voice*, Jan.16, 1998 p.9-10), we paid tributes to Poliakov for his intellectual honesty to speak out the historical truth and thereby diagnosing the disease but at the same time failing to cure the same. In other words, Poliakov also proved wrong in finding fault with us for describing India's Aryan *vaidiks* as the "Jews of India". And here also we proved right.

Now, yet another revealing book has just been published in the United States further supporting our choice of words describing India's fascist and fanatical Aryan *vaidik* forces as "Hindu nazis".

The words "Hindu nazis" were coined by us after a good deal of trial and error. For over a decade we were not able to get the exact words and phrases to picture these enigmatic creatures who indeed are a wonder of the world.

The fascist and fanatical Aryan upper castes (Hindus) have neither any common name, nor organisation, political party nor a grouping. Not all members of the Hindu nazi terrorist organisation, Rashtriya Swayamsevak Sangh (RSS), are fanatics and fascists.

Hundreds of innocent SC/ST/BCs doped and duped by *vaidik* forces have become foot-soldiers of the RSS and die in nazi-inspired war and violence. They may be members of the RSS but how can we call them Hindu nazis? Sister Uma Bharati may be a member of the *Brahmana Jati Party* (BJP) but we can't call her Hindu nazi because she is blood of our blood, bone of our bone.

Nazis in marxist parties

Much more dangerous persons can be found in the Congress, the original brahminical party of India, and even in communist parties. Many pious-looking persons parading as gandhians are deadlier than cobras.

Fascist and fanatical upper castes, who stand for all anti-human values, conveniently divide themselves and get distributed in all parties and organisations. Some work as scientists and human rights advocates and even communist leaders. S.A. Dange, founder-chairman of India's Communist Party, and E.M.S. Namboodiripad, the "Modern Shankara", are good examples of Hindu nazis found in marxist parties.

So, in DV we were finding it difficult to give them one single name. If we identify them with their organisational name like RSS or BJP, then we will be leaving out more dangerous *vaidiks* like the ex-Prime Minister, P.V. Narasimha Rao.

The just published book by a White Western Christian scholar, Nicholas Goodrick-Clarke, *Hitler's Priestess, (Savitri Devi, the Hindu Aryan Myth & Neo-Nazism*), is the best document that we have so far received fully endorsing the choice of our words, "Hindu nazis", to describe India's hate-mongering brahminical forces. DV once again proved right.

Like the philosopher of German nazism, Nietzsche, this French Christian woman also rejected her religion of Christianity and embraced Brahminism and married a Brahmin. (*Dalit Voice*, April 16, 1997: "*Why Nietzsche rejected Christianity & followed Brahminism?*" and Oct.1, 1996 p.10: "*Nazi philosopher Nietzsche borrowed from Brahminism*", Raju Thomas).

Goodrick-Clarke's book answers the question that we raised: *Who is the Mother of Hitler?* (1984-DSA). The mother is Brahminism, the founding father of racism, fascism, nazism and also zionism.

DV welcomes "Clash of Civilisations"

Savitri Devi, the French woman's adopted name, fell in love with the Aryan hate-mongering racist philosophy, married a Bengali Brahmin and wrote many books commending the White Western people to come to India and study its Aryan philosophy. This Aryan-Hindu Mother of Hitler died on Oct.22, 1982 in England leaving a "profound" influence on the Western thought.

Her influence proved so decisive and all-pervading that America's top Jewish scholar, Samuel Huntington, came out with his deadly hate-mongering thesis: "Clash of Civilisations", predicting victory of the West over the rest. (*Dalit Voice* Editorial March 1, 1998: "*DV Welcomes Clash of Civilisations*").

Savitri Devi's original name was Maximiani Portas (1905). A French woman of Greek-English birth, she soon became an admirer of Hitler's nazism and got obsessed with the Aryan Myth.

The sole credit for promoting and perfecting Hitler's nazism that allegedly killed millions of Jews and caused two World Wars goes to this diabolical Aryan brahminical thought as propounded in the Vedas and all their Sacred Scriptures. Naturally, all hate-mongering racists made a beeline to India and Ms. Portas also came to India, the original home of racism.

Nazis join hands with zionists

Today's White Western racists may not hate the Jews. Rather, the two have joined hands to target their new enemies — the Blacks, Muslims and India's Black Untouchables (Dalit Voice, Editorial March 16, 1988: "*White Western racists & zionists launch their civilisational war against Islam & China*"). This is the latest development and enough has been written on the "Huntington's Civilisational Clash", the latest high priest of Hitler.

Aryans born to rule world

Ms. Portas like many other racist Whites fell in love with the Aryan *vaidik* philosophy which revealed her that the White Western Europeans (Nordics) and India's Aryans are racially one and born to rule the world.

The Aryan-manufactured caste system, based on *varna* (skin colour), which is the foundation on which the brahminical social superiority is built, ideally suited the White European race. This racial superiority of the Whites made them develop their Apartheid rule in South Africa. And the same philosophy of *Varnashrama Dharma* (the Indian brand of Apartheid) made the Aryan *vaidiks* to develop their Hindu nazism to rule over India.

Savitri Devi went to Rameswaram in Tamil Nadu, and visited all "holy" Hindu centres. She even lived (1935) with Tagore, a Bengali Brahmin, at Bolpur and learnt Bengali.

Tilak says Aryans are foreigners

She was profoundly impressed by B.G. Tilak, one of the founding fathers of Hindu nazism.

Tilak's book, *The Arctic Home in the Vedas*, in which India's topmost Brahmin scholar acknowledges the foreign origin of India's Aryans, had profound influence on her. It is in this book Tilak says Aryans do not belong to India and hence not its original inhabitants — a theory which today's Hindu nazis are desperately trying to refute but failed.

M.S. Golwalkar, the philosopher of the Hindu nazi party, also said that the "Arctic home of the *vedas* was verily Hindustan", thus acknowledging the foreign origin of his fellow Aryans. (*Dalit Voice* April 16, 1993 p.22: "*Nazi party founder says invading Aryans brought Hinduism*"). The philosopher of Hindu nazi party admits that Hinduism is a foreign religion in his book, *Hindu Rashtra Darshan*, 1992.

Historians Neelakanta Shastri and Srinivasachari, both Brahmins, have also said that Aryans came from Iran. (*Dalit Voice* Dec.16, 1992 p.22).

The Bengali *Bhadralok* culture, which was the forerunner of today's Hindu nazi thought process, impressed Savitri Devi so much that she initially fell in love with not only Bengali but married a Bengali Brahmin, Asit Krishna Mukherji (1940).

How to love both Hitler & British

She was gradually getting absorbed into RSS thoughts. Her favourite icons were Veer Savarkar, Tilak, Dr. Hedgewar. And also Adolf Hitler.

Look at the irony: While India's English-educated upper castes were occupying top positions in the then British Government and also great admirers of the British, they were secretly admiring Hitler against whom the British had waged two World Wars. Treachery, thy name is Brahminism — nay Hindu nazism.

The German nazi rulers maintained clandestine connections with top brahminical leaders, writers and administrators of those days.

Why this double-face? This is natural with Brahminism. Some times it has more than two faces. It may be three or even four faces, depending upon the advantage the *vaidiks* derive. Brahminism can admire Hitler and his nazism and at the same time dine, dance, eat and sleep with zionism, the enemy of nazism.

The entire White Western racists are today making a beeline to India to study "Indian philosophy". Satya Sai Baba, Krishna Consciousness (ISKON), Yoga and many other forms of bullshit took birth exactly for this reason.

Dying race

The over-fed White Western racists, a dying, decaying race because its population is fast falling, knows that its new-won prosperity is due to its hegemony over the whole world. All hegemonists are in a minority and hence feel threatened.

The White Western rulers (there are many saner elements among the White Westerners who are an exception to the rule) need not worry about anything. They possess everything. Yet they feel threatened. A psychological fear has gripped them. They see danger haunting at every corner. Thinking sections among them do not get even sound sleep in the night.

It is this fear in the White Western racist mind that has produced a Samuel Huntington. And such Huntingtons come to India in search of "peace". And they found it in Hindu nazism, the mother of Hitler. DV has proved right.

(*Dalit Voice*, Editorial April 16, 1999).

ANNEXURE - 4

Casteism (Brahminism) as World's Worst Form of Racism

Speech delivered at the VII Session of the "Global Conference Against Racism and Caste-Based Discrimination" on March 3, 2001 at the Nehru Memorial Library building, Teen Murti, New Delhi, organised in preparation for the "UN World Conference Against Racism (WCAR), Durban, South Africa, in September 2001.

As the Editor of *Dalit Voice*, the country's oldest and the largest circulated Dalit journal and the "*Voice of the Persecuted Nationalities Denied Human Rights*", we have a very long and rewarding experience in fighting casteism, the Indian brand of racism which has religious sanction under Hinduism.

You may be surprised to hear that it was *Dalit Voice* which announced as far back as 20 years that casteism or Brahminism is racism. And that racism was exported from India by the Aryans. And that Brahminism is the founding-father of racism, fascism, nazism, zionism.

We have written several books on this subject, translated to German, Japanese and French languages.

Hitler's nazism was inspired by Brahminism. All the German philosophers of nazism and even Max Muller had acknowledged it. India's Aryan brahminical forces hailed Hitler as an *avatar* incarnation of god) and gifted their swastika to Hitler. Swastika mark is found at the very entrance to every Brahmin and other upper caste house in India.

Passport impounded

When the Afro-Americans (Blacks) learnt that India is the original home of racism, they came to India in hundreds. American Black scholars are convinced that racism was exported from India and that India has the world's largest racially oppressed people called the Dalit — the Black Untouchables. And I must have so far received at least 50 American Black delegations in the past 20 years.

I have written a book, *DALIT-The Black Untouchables of India,* Published from the US (Clarity Press, Suite 469, 3277 - Roswell Rd., N.E., Atlanta, GA.30305, USA), and it has gone into third edition though India's brahminical "national" toilet papers have refused to give any publicity to this book.

For announcing to the world that Brahminism is the founding father of racism, fascism, nazism, and that racism was exported to the world from India, India's ruling Brahminical Social Order (BSO) amply rewarded me by impounding my passport way back in 1986.

For the past 15 years I am not allowed to go out of India. And yet the BSOsays that India is the "largest working democracy in the world". Bullshit. (*cheers*).

Fake human rightwalas

By keeping me out, all international conferences have been captured by fake human *rightswalas,* most of them upper caste. And these upper caste human *rightswalas* are misleading the outside world, cunningly suppressing the fact that India's human rights problems are caused mainly because of caste and casteism. The organisers of this conference should be careful that you too are not hijacked by these fake human *rightswalas.* (*cheers*).

Apart from impounding my passport, I was arrested half a dozen times including under TADA, MISA, Sedition etc. Two attempts were made on my life. Twice I was sent back from Delhi where I shifted in 1990 and 1998. This is the meaning of Hindu tolerance, compassion, non-violence, *Satyameva Jayate.* (*cheers*).

Not even the Peoples Union for Civil Liberties (PUCL) took any interest in my passport, arrest, persecution because all our human rights organisations are also Brahmin-dominated. The president of the PUCL, also a Brahmin, is sitting here and he knows it. If the South African Blacks were victims of violence, we Dalits in India are the victims of non-violence of the M.K. Gandhi brand. (*cheers*).

The South African Apartheid pales into insignificance before the Indian brand of racism. Even in the Gujarat earthquake relief, now underway, the rulers have practised racism. Western aid-givers have themselves complained about it.

Fair-looking girls

The Sanskrit name for racism is *Varnashrama Dharma*. And "*varna*" means colour, skin colour.

Nowhere in the world so much of importance is given to skin colour as in India. Dark-looking people are looked down upon. Look at the matrimonial columns in leading "national" dailies. Everybody wants a fair-looking girl. (laughter).

And the Untouchables of India are the darkest-looking people.

Plight of President Narayanan

To counter our argument, the ruling Aryan racists will give the example of a dark-skinned Dalit elevated to the position of the highest office, President, K.R. Narayanan.

I have met him twice. Poor man is living in a vast 100-bed room jail called the *Rashtrapati Bhavan*, with no power and daily ridiculed in the brahminical media. (*Mainstream*, Feb.10, 2001 p.11).

The subject matter of this conference is so vast and so important because we are dealing with the world's most ancient and also the world's deadliest enemy with a religious garb. But we have no time to elaborate.

I request the organisers to evolve foolproof strategies and

tactics and fight this enemy at Durban and on behalf of *Dalit Voice* and its family world-wide we wish you all success. Thank you for your honour done to us. You must know that you are fighting an uphill task. The problem is over 3,000-year-old.

Defeat of Budhism

Brahminism defeated the most powerful religion like Budhism itself and drove it-out of India.

Fighting casteism and racism means fighting Brahminism which today has joined the White Western racists and zionists and has become a world force after developing global contact.

So, please don't dilute the issue by mixing up so many things. It is not an ordinary enemy you are facing.

While it is our duty to fight Brahminism in the interest of saving India and the world, I want to impress upon you that our battle has to be fought essentially within India where our people are getting fast *hinduised* or brahminised.

So, while impressing the United Nations to equate casteism (not caste) with racism, I request you to concentrate more inside India, where our main battle has to be fought.

(*Dalit Voice*, April 1, 2001 p. 8-9).

ANNEXURE - 5

When the "Axis of Evil" met at Durban

The just concluded UN World Conference Against Racism (WCAR) equating zionism with racism and declaring the Jewish state of Israel as a "racist, apartheid state" at its Durban session on Sept.3, 2001 is a big victory for *Dalit Voice*.

Because we were the first in the world to describe the Brahmins as the "Jews of India" and also announce that Brahminism is the founding father of racism, fascism, nazism and zionism.

Unique people in the world

Our description of the Aryan Brahmins as the "Jews of India" was criticised by some scholars.

The most important characteristic common to both Brahmins and Jews is that through religious conversion one **cannot** become a Brahmin or Jew. Any one can become a Christian, Muslim or Budhist through conversion. But a Brahmin or Jew is one who must be a born Brahmin or born Jew. This marks the Brahmin and the Jew as a unique people in the whole world. No other religion in the world has this special characteristic.

The religion of both, if it can be called a religion, is based on hate-mongering, racism and violence.

That India's Hindu nazi ruling class led by its Brahmins opposed the WCAR resolution at Durban dubbing Israel as racist state and Israel praised the Brahmin support. This further proves that the two think alike and act alike. The zionists supported the Brahmins at Durban and vice-versa.

We are, therefore, fully justified in describing Brahminism as the mother of racism, fascism, nazism and zionism.

Both India's brahminical leaders living in and outside India and international zionist leaders are in close touch with each other since over 50 years. Israeli defence forces are guiding the India's defence force in fighting terrorism (read Muslims).

Hated Muslim leader

Durban conference has lifted the curtain on the hush-hush dealings between the two. India's brahminical rulers fielded a hated Muslim leader, Omar Abdullah of Kashmir, to plead for zionists at Durban.

All hate-mongers and anti-human fellows the world over are coming together under the leadership of USA. But the overwhelming world population, comprising the Blacks, the Black Untouchables of India, Muslims and China plus some fair-minded White Western people are on the side of Justice, Truth and Human Rights.

The just concluded Durban conference has revealed the true colour of the so-called democracy-mongers led by the USA. India's tiny Aryan brahminical rulers have jumped on the American bandwagon in their hatred of indigenous Dalits and Muslims. The "Clash of Civilisations" as outlined by Samuel Huntington in his book of the same title is getting more pronounced.

The Aryan Brahmins are assuming almost world leadership of this current war against all oppressed races. As the founding father of racism, fascism, nazism and zionism, it is but natural that they should take this leadership.

(Report in *Dalit Voice* Oct.1, 2001 p.8).

BY THE SAME AUTHOR

1.	Basavalingappa's Rationalist Battle	(1974)
2.	Conspiracy Behind Communal Riots (A study of India's Muslim Problem)	(1977)
3.	Havanur & The Bible of the Backward Classes	(1977)
4.	Crocodile Tears over "Harijan" Atrocities	(1978)
5.	"Harijan" Atrocities — Why Blame Police?	(1978)
6.	Dalit Sahitya (Kannada)	(1978)
7.	Apartheid in India	(1978)
8.	Dalit Movement in Karnataka	(1978)
9.	The Relevance of China	(1980)
10.	Tribal Unrest — Whom to Blame?	(1980)
11.	Class-Caste Struggle: Emerging Third Force	(1980)
12.	Untouchability — Can it Be Removed?	
13.	How to Destroy Caste System?	(1981)
14.	Brahminism (The Curse of India)	(1981)
15.	Who is Ruling India	(1982)
16.	The Agony of Being a Muslim	
17.	Hinduisn vs the Movement of Untouchables in India	(1983)
18.	Dr. Ambedkar & His Conversion	(1983)
19.	The Dilemma of Class & Caste in India	(1984)
20.	Who is the Mother of Hitler?	(1984)
21.	Hinduism, Fascism & Gandhism	(1985)
22.	The Birth Pangs of Khalistan	(1985)
23.	A Recipe For Revolution	(1985)
24.	The Hindu Demand for Common Civil Code	(1986)
25.	Who Made the Muslims "Communal"?	(1986)
26.	Muslims & the Liberation of the Oppressed	(1986)
27.	Merit, My Foot	(1987)
28.	The State Used to Promote Hindu Religion in India ?	(1987)
29.	Muslims to Divide Muslims: Hindu Nazis' Latest Trick	(1987)
30.	How Marxh Failed in Hindu India	(1988)

31. Karl Marx & Dr. Babasaheb Ambedkar (1988)
32. Mahatma Gandhi & Babasaheb Ambedkar (1989)
33. Dr. B.R. Ambedkar's Three Commandments: Educate, Agitate, Organise — Its Essence & Consequence (1989)
34. Dr. B.R. Ambedkar's Three Commandments (1990)
35. Know the Hindu Mind (1990)
36. Ready Reference to Revolutionaries (1991)
37. Bangarappa, Victim of Brahminical Conspiracy (1992)
38. Brahmihism: Father of Fascism, Racism, Nazism (1992)
39. Dialogue of the Bhoodevadas (1993)
40. Dalit Movement in India (1994)
41. Defects of the Dalit Movement: Lacking in Strategies & Tactics (1995)
42. DALIT — The Black Untouchables of India (Published in the United States) (1995)
43. Separate Electorate & Separate Settlement (1996)
44. Why Godse Killed Gandhi? (1997)
45. Reservation Policy & Ambedkarism (1997)
46. India's Muslim Problem (1998)
47. India's Intellectual Desert (1999)
48. Brahminism Swallowing Ambedkar Movement (1999)
49. Christians & Dalit Liberation (2000)
50. The Second Partition of India (2000)
51. Aggression on Indian Culture (2001)
52. Grave Diggers of History (2001)
53. Caste — A Nation Within the Nation (2002)

Forthcoming books

1. India as a Failed State
2. Chandigarh Jail Yatra
3. Antidote to Globalisation